I've Always Stood Alone, but I'm Still Standing

by Linda J. Petersen

Chapbook Press

Schuler Books
2660 28th Street SE
Grand Rapids, MI 49512
(616) 942-7330
www.schulerbooks.com

I've Always Stood Alone but I am Still Standing

ISBN 13: 9781948237994

Library of Congress Control Number: 2021923989

Copyright © 2021 Linda J. Petersen

All rights reserved. No part of this book may be reproduced in any form except for the purpose of brief reviews or citations without the written permission of the author.

Printed in the United States by Chapbook Press.

I wish I could have had

a Mother and a Father,

a tub to bathe in

and hot, running water.

The only one whom I knew loved

me was my Great Grandmother.

Oh where, oh where were my mother and father?

My old school clothes from

last year,

my dad said I should mend

as I shed a tear.

Why is our family so poor?

All the other kids get more and more.

I didn't realize until later

it was alcohol abuse.

It took from us kids and put

our dad in a noose.

Later he died, so what was the use?

Linda J. Petersen, 1970s

*All I could see is the desperation in her eyes.
So empty, so hollow, such a demise.
If only she knew, life can be better.
But the addiction is there; it goes away but never.*

Linda J. Petersen, 1986

Table of Contents

Chapter 1: Innocent and Abandoned 1

Chapter 2: Too Soon for This 14

Chapter 3: Time to Move On 29

Chapter 4: No One Seems to Care, Including Me 37

Chapter 5: Looking to be Loved 43

Chapter 6: An Extremely Dangerous, Rotten Man 54

Chapter 7: One Night on Broadway 79

Chapter 8: Smothered 93

Chapter 9: The Right Thing to Do 101

Chapter 10: A Constant Joy 127

Chapter 11: Gone Too Soon 134

Chapter 12: My Soul Mate Experience 139

Chapter 13: Great Actor 148

Chapter 14: Alcoholic Crutch 169

Chapter 15: Prosecutors Perform Puppet Show 176

Chapter 16: My Only True Love 188

Epilogue 198

Foreword

I have been acquainted with Linda Petersen for 45 years. Over the years, I have observed some of the triumphs and hardships that she has had to live through. I consider Linda a free-spirited lady with an unbounded trust towards humanity. This has been her partial downfall, as well as her ability to endure. As many of us in life have discovered, not everyone has our best interests in mind.

I have learned over the years to admire her strength for all that she has experienced during her lifetime. Linda is a true pioneer of the human heart and perseverance. I feel really blessed to know Linda and call her a friend. Let the words in the pages of this book be a testimony for all that have ever had to struggle and overcome adversity.

Friends for life,

Norman

Chapter 1: Innocent and Abandoned

Up until I was eight years old, I was just a typical girl growing up in a lower-class home. I was born to Mae and David Holder on June 11, 1954, in Bay City, Michigan, and named Linda Jean Holder. I was a petite-framed girl with blue eyes and brown curly hair. My mother always had me wearing a dress with my flat round black-toed shoes with white-laced ankle socks. I was taught to say "please" and "thank you." My mom tells me that I was a good kid. I always minded, and I don't remember ever getting a spanking from either parent. I used to wait for the bus across the street from my house, little plaid book-bag in hand. I would be the first kid to be picked up, so I would sit right behind the bus driver. I enjoyed learning. I was a pretty good speller, and I liked when we had spelling bees. English, writing, and spelling were the classes I was the best in, but when I had to do a book report and stand in front of the class, I was petrified. I lacked self-confidence due to no emotional support or guidance from my parents. I didn't like being the center of attention. I enjoyed my gym class—especially when we played basketball, kickball, and volleyball. I really liked music, and it was my desire to learn how to play an instrument, but my dad couldn't afford it. Even though I didn't think I had a good singing voice, I sang in the choir class and outside while swinging to the Beatles song, "I Want to Hold Your Hand." I loved the Beatles, the Beach Boys, and the Four Seasons.

My mother got pregnant with me when she was 15 and my father was 19, and they got married before I was born. They were young, but they chose to get married because in the 1950s, having children out of wedlock wasn't widely accepted in society. I was the oldest of four children – my sister Deborah came next, then my brother Crockett, followed by my youngest sister Pam. We were all about a year apart in age.

Our home was on Boy Scout Road in a rural area of Bay City. It was nothing fancy, but it was home. The house had two bedrooms and a half-bath. There was a gas stove in the living room, the house's only source of heat during Michigan's cold winters. We used to huddle around it in the winter time and rub our hands together. We didn't have a water heater, either, so we used the kitchen stove to heat water to do the dishes, wash our hair, and bathe, which became a time-consuming process. Since we didn't have a bathtub, we had to take sponge baths in the small bathroom sink. I remember Deborah and I going outside whenever it rained to wash our hair. After a while, my dad finally bought a round metal silver tub for us to bathe in. Even with the new tub, it took so long to heat enough water to fill it that we would have to take turns using the same water.

We didn't have a washing machine, so my mom went to the laundromat to wash our clothes. She'd hang them on the line to dry in the summer. When I was 6 years old, I recall going to the laundromat with my mother. An old, small brick building, the laundromat had only 20 washing machines total. Machines with packets of powdered laundry soap, coin machines, snack, and pop machines filled the spaces not occupied by the laundry machines. While in the laundromat, my mom was busy taking the clothes out of the washers and putting them in the dryers. I was bored, and headed over to the coin machine. I slowly turned the machine's knob to the right, and to my surprise, a whole bunch of quarters rattled down. I thought I hit the jackpot. It was maybe five dollars in quarters, so I thought I was rich. Immediately, I scooped up the quarters and raced over to show my mom.

"Mom! Look! These came out of the machine over there. Can I keep them?"

She looked around the laundromat to see if they might have belonged to someone else, but no one else was there.

"You can keep one quarter for some candy, and I'll use the rest to dry the clothes."

"Okay, Mommy!"

Later that day, once all the laundry was done, she took me to the local store that we passed on our way home. The store had a basket of penny candy on the counter. I carefully went through it and selected each piece. When we got home, I shared my 25 treasures with my brother and sisters. Every time after that, when my mom had to do laundry, I asked to go with her in hopes of getting lucky again.

We might not have had much money, but the memories I had from my early childhood were happy. I spent as much time as possible outside in the yard or in the woods. On summer nights, we ran around catching lightening bugs in jars, catching tadpoles in the ditch, or grabbing onto the branches of the big willow tree in the front yard to swing across the ditch. When it rained, we would play in the mud puddles, and in the fall, we'd play in the leaves. In the wintertime, I'd build a snowman or maybe a fort and have snowball fights with my siblings. My dad hung an old tire on the biggest tree in the backyard for us to swing on, and we also had a swing set. I remember Deborah trying to be helpful one day by burning the trash. However, she didn't take the trash out to the barrel; she went to the corner of the kitchen and lit the paper bag of trash on fire. I saw what was happening I rushed to fill up my little pail and dumped it on the fire.

I got along with my mother when I was a child, even though she lacked affection and compassion. She was about 5'1" and had a petite frame with big hazel eyes and thick, wavy, black hair. She didn't like to cook, but she always made sure her house and her children were clean and well-mannered. However, she had moments when she put her cleaning before her children.

One time, Deborah, Crockett, Pam, and I were outside during the winter, and we were freezing cold. We wanted to come into the house, but she made us stay outside because she was cleaning.

I have several fond memories with my dad, more than I ever had with my mom. He was a small man, about 5'8" and 150 pounds with wavy light-brown hair, blue eyes, a clean-shaven face, and no glasses. His front top teeth were slightly bucked out. He used to wear white t-shirts with a pocket in the front, where he would keep his Pall Mall cigarettes, and blue jeans with pant-legs rolled up. My dad was working at a foundry doing sheet metal work during my early childhood. He used to wear these heavy steel-toed boots, and after a long day, his feet would get sweaty and smelly, so he would pay me a quarter to wash his feet for him in a plastic tub of hot water. In his leisure time, he would enjoy pheasant and deer hunting, and oftentimes, he would bring Crockett with him. When I was little, we had a dog named Tuffy; he was a medium-sized dog with short brown hair and floppy ears. Once when I was washing his food bowl, I asked my dad if it was clean enough.

He said, "Would you eat out of it?"

I said, "No."

"Then wash it again."

My parents were pretty good to me and my siblings during our early childhood, but I only have two memories of them spending any time alone together. Once when I was about 6, I woke up to use the bathroom and saw them sitting on the couch in the living room watching TV. Another time about a year later, they went to a drive-in movie. I remember my mom giving me the rest of the box of popcorn that she didn't eat. I don't remember them ever fighting, but I don't recall them ever being affectionate to one another either.

When I was in third grade, 8 years old, my mom left my dad and all four of her children. I was too young to really understand what was happening. I remember asking my dad, "When is mom coming home?" but I don't remember what his answer was. It was just clear that she was gone. I don't remember how I felt. I have suppressed my feelings to protect myself. I instinctively knew that I was in charge being the oldest, and I kept busy with my three heartbroken siblings. Eventually, my parents divorced. My dad was totally devastated at losing my mom. He had not wanted a divorce. He soon turned to alcohol and cigarettes and became emotionally unavailable.

In 1963, when I was nine years old, our great grandmother – my mother's grandmother – moved in with us. My dad needed somebody to help him with the four of us kids so he could work. Great-grandma Clarissa was short and overweight. Her short gray hair was often covered with a hairnet, which went nicely with her wide-framed glasses, like owl's eyes. A typical outfit for Great-grandma was a loose dress with a full under slip, which she called her petticoat. A small, silver cross was always safety-pinned right above her heart. Nylons, rolled up to just under her knees, and black, old-fashioned school teacher shoes completed the look. Her voice was rough—so rough, that she sounded like a man on the phone. Her masculine voice was probably due to her Pall Mall cigarettes.

I really loved my great-grandma. She instilled principles in me that I'll never forget. She taught me to always respect other people's things, no matter how old or new they were, and to keep what I had clean, and appreciate it. Great-grandma was very poor, but she was a giver. If she felt somebody needed what she had more than her, she'd give it to them. She was also a God-fearing woman. Every night before bed, she read her Bible. Even before she lived with us, Deborah and I would love to spend the night at Great-Grandma's house. We got to stay up late watching TV, and bedtime came when the news came on, marking 11 pm. She'd let me sleep in her bed, which was really fun, except for the scratchy, wool Army blankets. After moving in, my great-grandma filled the void that my mother had left, and she was more affectionate than my mother had ever been, so I cherished the time that she lived with us. She spent time with me and helped me with my studies.

While our great-grandma was living with us, my father married a woman named Sandy, who became my step-mother. Sandy was the total opposite of my mother in regard to appearance. She had short blonde hair and blue eyes, somewhat of a pointy nose, and bucked teeth. She didn't wear makeup and bit her fingernails extremely short. My dad's goal was to marry a woman who was happy with him and wouldn't leave him for another man, like my mother did. When my dad married Sandy, she was 19 and already pregnant. Sandy gave birth to a daughter, Laurie, on April 21, 1963, and now there were five children to take care of. We all liked Sandy at first, but when she moved in, Great-grandma moved out because there wasn't room for her. Without our great-grandmother present, Sandy had to take care of us.

Three years later, Sandy became pregnant again. She gave birth to her son Allen on June 12, 1966, which bumped the total to six children. As time went by, we realized that Laurie and Allen were treated better than us four step-children ever were. Sandy would buy her own kids new clothes, punish them less, and give them more food while her step-children were at school. Sandy wasn't much of a cook and food was scarce, but she would horde tuna in her dresser drawers for herself and her children. Once we started standing up for ourselves and complaining about her favoritism, Sandy started calling me "Brat" instead of calling me by name. My dad usually stood up for us, but he had to work, so there wasn't much he could do while he was gone.

I suppose Sandy did the best she could. After all, she was still a teenager when she married our dad. We had some quality family time together that I can remember fondly. When everybody was in the car, we'd all sing the song "Swing Low, Sweet Chariot" together. Sometimes, I would hang out with Sandy and her friend next door, who would bring me Avon lipstick samples.

As the oldest, I was given a lot of responsibility, especially because my dad and Sandy would drink and party constantly. When I would get home from school, they would take off and go to the bar, leaving me alone to take care of all five children. While she and our dad spent their money at the bar, we didn't even have toilet paper at home, so we used newspaper instead. Deborah and I would stay up late into the night ironing and watching TV. We would hear about race riots and claims of UFO sightings on the news, and we were so scared that we couldn't fall asleep. We'd stay up until we heard the national anthem on TV at 12 am before all three channels went off the air, then we would go to bed to avoid seeing Dad and Sandy stumble in from the bar.

On nights they didn't go to the bar, they'd have parties at the house. There would be multiple brown cardboard cases of beer in bottles and a house full of people drinking, smoking, and dancing until late into the night. We kept waking up because of all of the noise and we wouldn't be able to fall back to sleep. When the parties were over, there would be all of kinds of beer bottles and cigarette butts left in the ashtrays. Pam, 8 years old, and Crockett, 9 years old, used to drink the warm beer left in the bottles and smoke the cigarette butts, but Deborah and I never liked the taste of beer.

During one party, an old man – one of my dad's friends – got drunk and tried to kiss me. I was only 10 or 11 years old. I told my dad, and he confronted him. The man still came around our house, but I avoided him and he never tried anything again. That experience still affected me, and I realized later in life that that was the beginning of my sexual abuse.

Our poverty is one of the clearest memories of my childhood. I don't remember getting new clothes very often. We were mostly given hand-me-downs, and we would just have to wear what fit, whether the clothes were meant for boys or for girls. There were times when Deborah and I would go to JC Penneys and steal clothing, only because we had no other means. Whenever we did this, my heart would start racing and I would be sweating. When we came out of the dressing room wearing stolen clothes under our own clothes, I would nonchalantly look around to see if anyone was onto us, and then we would put some of the clothes back and dash out the door. My dad eventually went to the state for financial help, so we were able to get hot lunch at school for free. I remember feeling so embarrassed standing in line without any lunch money and telling the teacher, "Hot lunch," even though I knew that was the best meal I would get for the day. I never wanted to invite friends over because of we lacked the basic household necessities and functions that my friends would have taken for granted. At school the other kids referred to us as the poor little Holder kids. All of these factors led to a very low self-esteem. My father had become more closed off after my mother left, so I never remember being told by anyone that I was pretty. I remember one time, looking at myself in my great grandmother's tarnished mirror, and telling myself that I thought I was pretty.

Regardless of my family's lack of money, I had a decent relationship with my father while I lived with him. I felt that I could talk to him about most things, and he was easy to get along with and he had a sense of humor. On one occasion, I was in my bed sleeping and when my dad decided it was time to wake me up, he poured water into my ear. I woke up all right, and when I felt the water, I instinctively lashed out toward his bare chest and scratched him with my long fingernails to the point of drawing blood. He didn't wake me up like that again. On another occasion, I was in the bathroom applying my mascara. While I was putting on the makeup, I had my mouth slightly open. My dad saw me and asked, "Are you putting that stuff on your eyes or your mouth?"

Sometimes I'd go along with him to the bar, and we'd dance with my feet on his feet. I really enjoyed that, and at least that way I got to spend some time with him. Another time, my dad and I were sitting on the bed together talking. We were horsing around and he rolled with me on the bed and told me he loved me. That's the only time I remember him telling me he loved me.

On my 16th birthday, he gave me a gold Timex watch. I do not remember receiving many gifts from my parents, making this watch very special. When he gave it to me, I was surprised that he acknowledged that important milestone in my life.

After my mother left, I hardly saw her until I was old enough to get in touch with her myself. My mom, Mae, was the third-born of five girls, and growing up, she was often the one who took the punishment for things that she didn't do. I think that the fact that she served as the whipping post for her siblings contributed to her lack of affection and emotion while raising us. My mother was quite rebellious in her youth, and at one point she was sent to juvenile hall. She gave birth to me when she was 16. I don't think that my mother was ready to be tied down with motherhood, and I'm assuming she felt overwhelmed having four children by age 20. I think that was the biggest reason she abandoned us. I only remember her coming over once when I was 13 because my dad told her I needed a bra, so she took me to go buy one. I remember really looking forward to seeing her that day. Other than that time, I never saw her or spoke with her.

Throughout my childhood, I used to like to spend the night at my grandparents' house. My Grandpa was my grandma's second husband, but he was the only Grandpa I ever knew. He never had any biological children of his own. Grandpa was 6'2," a thin man but his belly hung over his belt. He wore glasses and he was bald on the top of his head. He had really big ears, with hair growing inside of them. He used to call me "Ging" rather than Linda because he said when I would cry as a baby, it sounded like I was saying, "Ging, ging, ging!" Grandma was 4'11," overweight and bossy. She enjoyed riding a motorcycle, but never learned how to drive a car. Though she was kind to her grandchildren, I later found out she was very abusive to her husband and daughters, especially my mother. Regardless of the abuse, however, my grandparents remained married for the rest of their lives.

My siblings and I always thought our grandparents were rich because Grandpa worked for GM. They weren't rich, but they lived comfortably, and they moved around a lot. Grandpa would occasionally buy me suckers and comic books. I remember looking around their house for any spare change that my grandpa had dropped, and I would feel rich whenever he'd let me keep anything.

My best friend growing up was Barbara, who lived right across the street. She had light brown hair and blue eyes. She was slightly overweight, very kind, and loved animals. We went to different schools – I attended public school while she went to a Catholic school. I used to spend a lot of time over at her house. I got stuff over there that I never got at home, like hand-me-downs from Barbara's closet and home-cooked meals. Her mom always cooked and baked cakes. Every Sunday I'd go to church with Barbara and her family, and when we got back, we'd have dinner – usually Polish sausage and applesauce. I didn't understand a thing said in church because the priest was speaking in Latin. But that didn't matter – my goal was to eat.

Seeing how Barbara lived, I just wanted a normal life like hers. I knew as a young teenager that I was robbed of my childhood, and being in Barbara's house further reminded me of that.

Barbara and I liked swimming in her pool and drinking ice-cold Kool-Aid in the screened-in porch. On days that we left her house, Barbara and I would explore and make new paths in the woods. There, we found a secret hiding spot with a log perfect for sitting—and perfect for smoking.

When we were 10-years-old, Barbara and I would find beer and pop bottles in ditches and cash them in. Every time we got enough money for a pack of cigarettes – about 50 cents – we'd try a different brand. One day, we were in our secret hiding place, sitting on our log and smoking away. That day we were trying a pack of Kool's, a menthol cigarette. We both ended up choking and gagging. All of a sudden, we looked up and saw her brother and his friend. We hid the cigarettes behind our backs.

"This is our secret hiding place," Barbara said to her brother.

"Yeah, we can see that," he replied, noticing the smoke streaming up behind us.

He ran home and told his mother.

We both went home, and I could hear Barbara's mom yelling at her from across the street. I thought, "I'm really going to be in trouble when my dad gets home." Well, when he got home and found out about it, he confronted me.

"I heard you got caught smoking with Barb today."

"Yes."

That was the extent of the conversation. I didn't get punished, which was surprising. I think that hearing Barbara's mom give it to her scared me enough that I *never* tried smoking cigarettes again.

When we entered our teenage years, Barbara and I would go to basketball games, cruise around town, and get into trouble with boys. Barbara was seeing a guy nicknamed Chico, whose real name was Duane. I was 13-years-old when Chico introduced me to his friend Don, who was 17-years-old. Despite our age difference, we quickly started dating.

Don was an attractive young man. He was about 5'10" and 164 pounds. His dark brown hair was parted on the side and combed over, showing off his long sideburns that went down to the bottom of his earlobes. He had a mole on his cheekbone just below his eye. He also had a full, thick, nicely trimmed mustache. He was a practical joker, always goofing around and laughing. I thought his laugh was cute.

Dating Don was a whole new experience for me. I felt like I was starting a new life with him. Wanting desperately to escape my home life, I saw Don as a way out. His family lived in a nice, two-story home in Bay City. His mom worked at a sewing mill, and his dad was a salesman and was deeply involved with Knights of Columbus. They were an improvement from my family—supper on the table every night and toilet paper instead of newspaper.

Shortly after I began dating Don, I lived with my Aunt Beverly and Uncle Tim and their three children for a summer. I don't recall why I was living with them, but I suspect it was something I wanted to do to get away from all of adult responsibilities in my own home. Their home was a temporary place for me, but it was filled with amenities—food on the table, hot and cold running water, toilet paper, and clothing. No parties late into the night happened there like they did at my dad's house. Living with Aunt Beverly and Uncle Tim gave me more structure but not enough discipline. I asked my uncle to discipline me like his own daughter since I was living with them and wanted guidance. He commented that if I was his daughter, I wouldn't be seeing Don at all, but unfortunately, he didn't stop me.

Chapter 2: Too Soon for This

When the summer ended and the new school year started up, I moved back home. However, not long into the school year, my dad and Sandy moved across town, which placed my family home outside of my school's district. Deborah and I didn't want to switch schools in the middle of the year, so we moved in with my great-grandmother, Clarissa.

I was still dating Don, and things seemed to be going well with him. However, I had no kind of sex education. When I was going to school, that class didn't exist. I learned the hard way. In 1968, when I was 14, I woke up one day feeling very sick and threw up. I thought it was just a one-time thing, like the flu, but it kept happening every morning. I didn't know what was going on until I heard my great-grandma telling my dad on the phone that I was pregnant. When I heard what she'd said, I said to myself, "Oh, that's what's wrong with me."

When the news got back to my mom, she wanted me to go to a home for unwed mothers and give the baby up. I didn't want to do that, so Don and I got married on April 19, 1969, two months shy of my 15th birthday. We went to the judge's house in Bay City. I wore a navy-blue maternity dress with small white polka dots and a white, lace neckline. I had navy-blue nylons and white shoes, both of which were hard to put on since I was six months pregnant with swollen feet. Don wore a nice suit and tie. We wore matching pink carnation corsages. I wasn't wearing any makeup yet, since I was so young. After the wedding, we went to Don's parents' house to have some pictures taken and share a meal. There I was—14 years old, six months pregnant, bloated, and makeup-less. It certainly wasn't an ideal wedding photo, but it was one to remember.

About a month after I turned 15, I gave birth on July 13, 1969, to an 8-pound, 5-ounce baby boy, and I named him Daniel. Daniel was a healthy newborn with dark brown hair. He definitely had his dad's eyes—brown and squinty. He looked a lot like Don when he was a baby. The birth of my son Daniel made us a five-generation family. One day, when we were all together, a photograph was taken. My great-grandmother made it her personal goal to have that picture published in the local newspaper before she died, and her goal was fulfilled some months later. She passed away two years later in 1971.

After Daniel was born, Don and I lived with his parents temporarily until he got a job. He got into Saginaw Steering Gear, a GM plant, on the production line, which we were very happy about. If someone worked in the auto industry in Michigan, they had a good job. However, life was still difficult. A newborn and a husband working second-shift did not make for an easy time.

We lived like this for several months. Since Don was busy with work, I'd get bored, so I would take Daniel with me to visit Rich and his mom Janice, who lived right around the corner. Rich was Don's friend from high school who I'd met when Don and I had first started dating. He was about 18 at the time, and he was thin and quiet, with blond, curly hair and black-rimmed glasses. We'd play cards and eat dinner together. Janice liked me, and she enjoyed having a baby to hold. Sometimes, when I would go over there, Janice would be out of the house, so Rich and I started having sex. I knew that this was wrong because I was married to Don, but it wasn't really a planned action; it was just something that happened because I spent so much time over there. I was young and didn't have a lot of knowledge about marriage and commitment. Even so, I felt horribly guilty about it, and I ended the affair after a couple of months when Don and I moved into our own place a few miles away. We found a nice one-bedroom basement apartment on the west side of Bay City for $125 per month. Located behind a McDonalds, the apartment always smelled like French fries and hamburgers, which reminded me of summer.

While Don and I lived there, I found out that my stepmom, Sandy, was pregnant with her third child, and she gave birth to him on April 8, 1971, and named him Kenny. When he was born, he seemed to be healthy, but he was much thinner than he should have been. I wasn't able to spend a lot of time with him or get to know him very well because I was married and had my own child to look after.

What I didn't know about Don prior to marrying him was that he'd spent some time in juvenile hall, and I'm pretty sure it was for stealing. Despite the good job he had at GM, he still wanted to steal. One day, he said he wanted to do some B&Es – breaking and entering—and he needed a lookout, so he asked me. Of course, I didn't want to go, but I was afraid he'd get caught without someone to help him, so I reluctantly agreed to join him. We got a sitter for Daniel and found a house to break into. I was scared to death. What if someone happened to be home or come home? We got away from the first B&E without getting caught, and we did three more after that. We brought home stuff we thought we could sell – like typewriters, TVs, VCRs, and radios.

On our last B&E, the homeowners came home. I told Don that people were coming and we had to get out of there fast. As we were scrambling to get out, we accidentally left a patio door open, and they called the police. We walked down the road, trying to look unsuspecting, but we saw two police cars quickly approaching. We jumped into the deep ditch next to the road, but it was too late. We were both arrested.

I was 17 years old and Don was 21. Off to jail they took us, where I spent a total of five miserable days. There were three or four other women in the same cell as me. We all had to share the same toilet, and I caught crabs. It was the first venereal disease I'd ever had.

I hated jail, and I wanted out. I started screaming.

"Let me out of here!"

"If you keep that up, you'll end up down in the hole!" said one of my cellmates.

"What's that?"

"It's a cell without light. Solitary confinement."

Once I found that out, I stopped screaming. On the fifth day, they called my name and I was released. I never wanted to do anything to go back.

While I was in jail, I obviously didn't have my birth control pills with me so I started my period. Now my cycle was messed up, so I decided to go with the rhythm method of birth control. The problem was, I knew as much about my menstrual cycle and birth control as I did about becoming pregnant in the first place.

After I was released, I needed to talk to somebody about it, but Don was still in jail. I called Keith, a guy I went to school with, and we got together. I was scared of what was going to happen; I was crying, emotional, and vulnerable. Keith was trying to comfort me and we ended up having sex. We had sex just after I finished my period. As far as I knew, this was a "safe" time, so I wouldn't get pregnant.

Eventually Don was released awaiting trial, so he was able to come back home for a few weeks. Don was glad to be back home, and during that time we became intimate again. Of course, I missed Don, and I was happy he could spend that time with me, but I feared what the outcome of his trial would be. After all, I was a teenaged mother with no source of income. Don went to court and was sentenced to Jackson Prison. I broke down crying in the courtroom because I didn't know what I was going to do. After he got to prison, all I had to look forward to was getting a letter in the mail from him. The days slowly went by as I continued to live in the basement apartment, just me and Daniel. After a couple of months, I realized I wasn't having my period. I went to the doctor, who confirmed that I was pregnant again. I was happy and I was sad. My husband had just been sent off to prison, I was already raising one child, and now I was expecting another.

I went into labor on July 3, 1972. I gave birth to another baby boy. He was healthy, 7-pounds with light brown hair and blue eyes. While Daniel looked like Don, Steve looked more like me. I was happy that everything went well with the delivery and that we were both doing fine, but I was very disappointed that only two people came up to the hospital – Don's best friend Rich and his mother Janice. My in-laws didn't come to the hospital because they didn't believe the baby was Don's. I didn't know why they thought this because if they had done the math, they would have realized I got pregnant before Don went to prison, and no one knew about my fling with Keith.

With two young boys to take care of and a husband in prison, I was incredibly lonely and desperate for help and companionship. Because Don had gotten into so much trouble and he wasn't able to provide and support me with our children physically or emotionally, my feelings for him started to fade significantly. I didn't want to stay married to him when he was released from prison. With these feelings in mind, I reconnected with an older friend named Danny several months after Steve was born. He was in his early 20s, with brown hair, brown eyes, and a nice, full mustache. I was only 18 at the time, so even though I knew dating other men before getting divorced was technically wrong, I didn't want to wait for Don to be released from prison to have companionship. With all of these thoughts in mind, I decided to start dating Danny. After a few weeks, I found out he still had feelings for his ex-wife, so we stopped seeing one another.

Sometime before we broke up, Danny had introduced me to his brother Hugh, a handsome army man. Hugh had enlisted in the army right after high school, and he went to Vietnam and Germany twice. A purple heart recipient, he had recently come home from the Vietnam War; he was discharged as a Specialist E4 in March 1972. Don was still incarcerated, so I started dating Hugh. When I first met Hugh, he had short, well-kept hair, parted to the side and a nice full mustache. But since he was out of the army, he grew his hair down to his shoulders.

Hugh was living with his parents and his brother when he returned home, but shortly after we started dating, he moved into my one-bedroom basement apartment with me and my two boys. It was small but we made it work; I kept Steve's crib in the bedroom with Hugh and me. I had put up a three-panel room divider in the living room, and Daniel slept behind it. I was happy to have Hugh's help with Daniel and Steve, and Hugh got along with them very well. It was like apples to oranges—a thief to an army man.

I don't recall how my in-laws found out that Hugh was living with me because I made sure that he wasn't around when my in-laws came to see the boys, but they were very upset to find out. One time, my mother-in-law June and sister-in-law Julie came over and were questioning Daniel, asking him if there was another man staying with us in the apartment. I told them they had to leave. Not long after this, they started causing problems. Social services (now referred to as Child Protective Services) showed up at my door one day and wanted to see the boys. I was 18 years old, still young and naïve, so I let the man in. He looked at Daniel and was asking about a very small bruise he had on his leg. It wasn't anything to be concerned about, just what happens when a little boy plays and falls. After asking some questions, the CPS agent left. Not long after that, I decided to look for a bigger place, and Hugh, my two boys, and I moved into a townhouse in fall of 1972.

When Don was released from prison in the first couple months of 1973, he filed for divorce almost immediately. He found out that I had been dating and living with Hugh while he had been incarcerated, and he obviously wasn't happy about it. In all honesty, I was happy about the divorce because I didn't want Don to lead me into anymore criminal activities, and I wanted to set a good example for my boys and raise them in the best home environment possible.

On a Sunday in March 1973, Don came to pick up the boys for a visit with his parents. Our divorce was already in the works at this point, so we didn't spend time together at all anymore. Daniel was about 3 ½ and Steve was 8 months old. I gave Don the diaper bag with the things he needed, and he and the boys were gone for about five or six hours. Don brought them back later that afternoon. Shortly after they came back home, I needed to drive to K-Mart to get diapers, and when I was putting a hat on Steve to get him ready to go, he seemed a little fussy. I didn't see anything visibly wrong, so I didn't think much of it.

We got home from the store and ate dinner. Steve hadn't fussed or cried anymore that night, so I gave the boys a bath and put them to bed. At about midnight, I woke up to the sound of Steve crying. I assumed he was hungry, so I got up, warmed a bottle, and gave it to him without turning the light on, and he stopped. Before I even fell back to sleep, he was crying again, so I went to check on him more thoroughly. When I turned on the light, I was in total shock. His head was so swollen and big, it looked like a small melon.

I immediately woke Hugh up and we took Steve to the emergency room. The doctors asked me how this had happened, and I told them I didn't know – he had been completely fine when I had put him to bed. I was still in panic mode and deeply concerned for my baby, so I don't recall if I mentioned Steve fussing when I was putting on his hat earlier that day. I didn't think to mention to the doctors that Steve had been with his father most of the previous day. The doctors immediately assumed I had been abusing Steve and accused me right there in ER. I knew for a fact that I hadn't done anything, and knew Hugh hadn't either because I had been with him the whole time he was with the boys. I just couldn't explain what had happened.

The doctors said Steve needed to stay in the hospital until the swelling went down. I went to the hospital to see him every day, and it broke my heart to leave each time because he would cry and want to come home with me. After two days of treatment in the hospital, I went to see Steve I saw that he had a black eye and his testicles were swollen. My immediate thought was, "What the hell happened?" I didn't know how to explain any of this. After Steve was fully recovered, they wouldn't release him to me. I don't recall if they gave me a reason, but I knew he was perfectly fine at that point, and I missed my baby terribly and wanted him home. I went to the hospital, bundled him up, and we walked out the door.

The divorce proceedings were coming to a close; we just had a few more details to work out. Don wanted our 1972 Dodge Charger, and he also wanted full custody of Daniel only because his parents had convinced him that Steve wasn't his son.

In April 1973, when Steve was only 9 months old, a social worker came to my apartment and said he had been ordered to remove my boys from my home. I don't remember if he gave me a reason why that was happening, but I was in complete disbelief. The man gave me some paperwork which must have had official order on it because I remember reluctantly releasing Steve from my arms and into his. He hung onto Daniel's hand and held Steve as he left my apartment. I was so devastated after they were taken that I went to the bathroom to throw up.

It turned out that my sons had been taken from me over claims of child abuse. My ex-in-laws accused Hugh of abusing Steve and used him as a scapegoat in the situation. Once I heard their accusation, I knew they had set me up so Don could have custody of Daniel; he was their first grandchild, and he was their only goal. Don and my ex-in-laws knew that Steve sustained an injury, whether accidental or intentional, and withheld that information when they returned the boys to my care. Therefore, I looked like a liar and an abusive, neglectful mother. Hugh knew he was innocent, but he decided it was best if he moved back in with his parents until the situation was resolved. Don's father hired a very expensive, top-notch attorney to take me to court over custody of Daniel. I was only 18 and still living on welfare, so I couldn't afford an attorney. I was appointed a legal aid attorney named Mr. Blackman who did the bare minimum by telling me to only answer the questions I was asked without any elaboration.

I don't remember all of the details about the court hearing because I have repressed the memory for decades, but I do remember that when I was called to the witness stand, the judge asked me what had happened to Steve that caused his injuries, and I told him I didn't know because I truly didn't.

He stated, "They were in your care. You should know."

I didn't think I was allowed to bring up the fact that Steve had been with his father that day before the first injury had appeared, or that bruises don't always show up immediately and can sometimes take days to become visible. I was nervous, scared, and intimidated because I was only a teenager; I'd never been to court before, so I was intently following all of my attorney's instructions.

I was also alone. My family – including my closest sister Deborah, my four aunts, and my own mother – all went to court against me. None of them had asked me what had happened or what I thought might have happened. They believed that Hugh was abusing my children, and that I was choosing his companionship over the safety of my sons.

When Deborah was called to the stand, she told the court that I had been smoking marijuana in the presence of my children. This was true, but the only way Deborah knew that was because she often came over and smoked with me. I couldn't believe that she had said this to testify against me. Until this point, Deborah and I had been very close, so hearing those words was like a stab through my heart. Also, keep in mind, I was a teenager with little education and I wasn't aware of any negative side effects of second-hand marijuana smoke. In the 1970s, there wasn't even much research done into the negative impacts of smoking cigarettes and drinking alcohol while pregnant, so there was no way I would have known about second-hand smoke. If I would have known about any negative side effects, I never would have smoked weed in the house.

Even though my family members and my ex-in-laws all accused Hugh of hurting Steve, Hugh was never summoned to court or questioned by anyone about the situation. The court never brought up the fact that Don had a criminal record and had just been released from prison a few months prior. Don's father was a very prominent member of Bay City, and he a lot of connections. A little teenage nobody like me stood no chance against him and his top-notch attorney.

With no support of any kind, even from my attorney, the judge ruled against me because I couldn't explain what had happened. His decision was to severe my rights as a mother.

I didn't know what the word "severed" meant, so once the judge hit his gavel, I turned to my attorney and asked, "When can I see my boys again?"

My attorney told me, "You can't – your rights were severed. You're cut off. You can't see them ever again." The emotional pain in that moment was so unbearable that I remember I bellowed out a blood-curdling scream right there in the courtroom.

My attorney then continued, "But don't worry, you can have more kids someday." That comment left me speechless. I was so unbelievably distraught that I didn't even respond to him; I just turned around and walked away. I was an emotional wreck and I just wanted to go home. As I was driving, my eyes were so flooded with tears that I could hardly see. I returned to my now-empty apartment.

I couldn't believe what had happened. I'd just lost custody of my two baby boys and I had no one to provide emotional support and comfort. Hugh was still living with his parents and my family had abandoned me. I was so distraught that I couldn't eat, and when I was able to eat, I would throw up. Before this happened, I weighed 105 pounds, but in just a short period of time, I was in the low 90s. My face was thin, my cheeks were sunken in, and my clothes were now too big. I didn't know what to do with myself. I would just cry, look around, and cry some more, with nobody to call and no place to go. The whites of my eyes were completely red, surrounded by dark circles and puffiness. My nose was red, raw and stinging. The pain that I experienced at that time was unimaginable – it was like someone put their hand down my throat, grabbed ahold of my heart, and pulled it up, making me choke. I felt like I was missing limbs from my own body. The loss of my babies was the worst kind of pain a mother could ever feel, and I was forced to get through it alone, not knowing how I possibly could.

Since Don didn't think Steve was his son, he didn't want custody of him, so he was placed in foster care for 18 months. I remember receiving a single phone call from the woman who was taking care of Steve. I wanted so much to find out where he was and go get him, but I couldn't. As the days went by, I got more and more depressed. I couldn't handle staying in the apartment any more looking at the empty crib and bed, so I moved to a smaller, two-bedroom apartment.

At this point, I had already lost my entire world, so I didn't have anything left to lose. I didn't feel any kind of self-worth and my self-esteem was non-existent. I didn't really care what happened to me anymore. I felt like a failure as a mother, daughter, wife, sister, niece, and girlfriend, and I didn't know how to even begin healing, so I wallowed in those feelings. I became a risk-taker. I developed a carefree, promiscuous attitude and told myself that I'd try anything once, maybe twice.

I didn't know what else to do now that I was completely alone and without purpose, so I turned to sex, drugs, and rock 'n roll. To deal with the emotional pain, I would smoke weed. In the spirit of apathy, I also used blotter acid, mushrooms, mescoline, Quaaludes, black beauties, cocaine, and alcohol. If it would take me into the deep recesses of my mind and give me some semblance of peace, I would try it. My goal was to get as far away from reality as possible. My music choices became heavier, so I listened to albums like Led Zeppelin, Jimi Hendrix, and Pink Floyd.

Don eventually changed his mind and took Steve back. I found out later that I would have been able to visit the boys if Don would have let me, but when he got remarried, his wife didn't want him in contact with me at all. Don brought the boys over to see me one more time for about an hour. I hugged Steve and Daniel and kissed them while I was able. I had Don take pictures because I didn't know if I would ever be allowed to see them again. I later learned that Don's new wife, Wanda, who already had six children of her own, was abusive to my boys. Don had started drinking heavily and constantly once he was released from prison, and he became an alcoholic soon after. It was unbelievable that my in-laws and my family thought my boys would be better off living in an abusive environment with an alcoholic dad.

My relationships with a lot of my family members and Don's family members never fully recovered because of this incident. They all knew I was innocent. I still stayed in contact with my sister Pam and brother Crockett because they hadn't gone to court against me, so there were no hard feelings there. Over seven years later, Deborah sent me a letter apologizing for testifying against me in court, but I threw it away because I didn't think it seemed sincere. Don Sr. also contacted me years later to tell me that my ex-husband, Don, was back in prison and to apologize to me for what they had done. I told him it was all water under the bridge even though I was still carrying the irreparable pain of that incident. Don Sr. passed away shortly after that call.

In December of 2008, a few decades later, I heard that my ex-mother-in-law, June, had been diagnosed with leukemia. I knew that this might be my final chance to find out what had really happened to Steve, so I went to see her. I didn't want to jump right into the topic, but after about five minutes of small talk, I said straight out, "June, please tell me what happened to Steve."

She looked at me, propped her right fist under her chin, and looked away from me as she answered, "If I knew, I would tell you."

I knew she was lying, but I also knew by her response that she was going to take the truth to her grave. What interested me was that, even though she had told the court that Hugh had been the one abusing Steve, she never mentioned Hugh's name that day to accuse him again.

I told her that I'd come back in a couple of days to see her and said, "Maybe you might remember something."

We said our goodbyes, and as I was leaving the room, she said, "I love you."

I knew she felt horribly guilty, and regardless of my broken heart, I didn't want her to die with those feeling, so I turned back around and said, "I love you, too."

A couple of days later, I received a call from Don Jr. and he told me that I had upset his mother, so she didn't want me to visit her anymore. I knew she only told him this because she didn't want me to ask what had happened to Steve again. It was clear that she was doing everything she could to keep me from finding out the truth. June died shortly after my visit. A few years later, simply because I had the opportunity, I asked Keith to take a DNA test to ensure that Steve wasn't his son. As I had expected, the results came back with a 0.00% blood relation between Keith and Steve. Don Jr. heard about this and was upset that I sowed doubt in Steve's mind about who his father really was, clearly not caring that he was the one who had put Steve in foster care for 18 months because he had the same doubt. Just like his mother, Don refused to tell me what had really happened to Steve back in 1973, and he passed away on

November 18, 2018. With both ex-in-laws and my ex-husband gone, I have no hope of knowing who really abused my son.

The loss of my boys is still an open wound. Even now, when I'm home alone and reflect back, I become emotional and begin to cry. I know I can't change the past. When I am overcome with the memories of that time in my life, I tell myself, "Well, it's time to go roll one."

Chapter 3: Time to Move On

After the court case involving the custody of my boys was over, Hugh moved back in with me in my new apartment. Hugh and I stayed in one bedroom, and I set up the boys' beds in the other bedroom, still hoping for their return. Don and my family started to harass Hugh and me because Don was angry that I had started seeing Hugh while he was still in prison. On one occasion, Don called the police and told them we were in possession of marijuana. The police showed up and took everything they could find. They wanted to arrest us, but told us they would let us go if I would narc on someone else. The only person I knew who would have weed in his possession was someone I had gone to school with and known my whole life. I used to have a crush on this guy back in the third grade, but I ratted him out. After he got busted, he confronted me, and – of course – I denied it. I felt terrible.

The relationship between Hugh and me seemed to be going really well. We would often hang out with another couple, Karen and Bob, and play cards with them, especially in the winter months. Things seemed pretty good until I found out that Hugh had been cheating on me with Karen. I was extremely disappointed and hurt by this. I ended our relationship, and Hugh moved back in with his parents. He apologized, and we still talked from time to time, but I didn't want to live with him anymore because my trust in him was gone.

One evening, I went out by myself to Bay Lanes, a local bowling alley, to listen to live music. I was sitting at a table sipping a drink and enjoying the music. I was asked to dance several different times, and I did. Finally, the bar was doing last call, so I decided it was time to go. As I was driving, I noticed there was a car right behind me that appeared to be following me, and I was scared. Instead of going back to my apartment, I headed to Hugh's parents' house. On the way there, the person following me was flashing his high beams and honking his horn. I thought maybe something was wrong with my car and that he was trying to let me know, so I pulled over to the side of the road. He got out and approached my window. I rolled down my window to ask what was wrong.

The guy had just enough room to squeeze his arm through my window, and he unlocked and opened my door. I suddenly realized there wasn't anything wrong with my car. He wanted me instead. He told me to slide over. He got in my car, parked it a little further to the side of a road, grabbed my keys from the ignition, and made me get into his car.

He steered with his left-hand and held onto me with his right hand. He drove a black El Camino. I didn't notice anything else about him because I was so scared. He told me that he had been watching me all night, and he wanted me, meaning he wanted sex, but for fear of rejection, he didn't approach me at the bar. During the ride, I was planning my escape. Before he had decided where to take me, I told him that I was heading home, which was a lie. We were almost to Hugh's parents' house when he had pulled me over, so we kept driving in that direction.

He pulled up in the driveway and we got out, but he kept my keys in his hand. As we approached their back porch, which is the entrance everyone uses, I noticed the bathroom light was on. I yelled at the top of my lungs, "Hugh!" Then I heard a voice from the lit bathroom saying, "What the hell is going on out there?" It was Hugh's dad. When the guy heard that, he took off running back to his car, still holding my full set of keys. I never saw him again. The next day, Hugh took me to get my car and get my locks on my apartment changed.

That man put a lot of fear into me that night. I didn't know how closely he had been watching me; he might have written down the make and model of my car and my license plate number so he could find out where I lived. He might have still been stalking me for all I knew. I was constantly looking over my shoulder, and I never went back to Bay Lanes again.

I had been working a lot of odd jobs over the years to scrape by, but I wanted to find something a bit more stable. I applied for work at a local grocery store—Ray's Food Fair. I was a cashier, and I started out at $4.02 per hour. In the early seventies, that was pretty good money. I enjoyed working with the public and running a cash register.

One day a friend of my ex-mother-in-law came into the store. She knew about the court case and that I had lost custody of my boys. As if that wasn't already bad enough, she made things worse for me by filling in the manager. As a result, I got fired. It was apparent to me at that point that I couldn't have a life in Michigan anymore. I contemplated either going into the service or moving to California, but I decided on California because of a connection I had there.

Prior to Hugh moving out, he had introduced me to Marcia. She had long, brown, straight hair and brown eyes, and she never wore any makeup. She was about 5' 5" and thin. We got along right away. We were both Geminis, liked a lot of the same music, food, card games, coffee, and smoking weed. She was always upbeat and smiling.

Marcia was from my hometown of Bay City, Michigan. She had moved to California and was visiting Michigan because she and her husband Bob were having marital problems, so she stayed with me for a few months while she was sorting things out. Before she returned home to California, she told me that if I ever wanted to come to California that I could stay with her and Bob. She had a couple of cats but no children. In May of 1975, I decided it was time to go.

Prior to my move, I went and saw my dad one more time. He had put on some weight; his stomach was distended and his face looked swollen. I didn't think he looked well. I had a picture taken of the two of us. That ended up being the last time I saw him alive.

When the time came to move, I went to the bank and got $400 worth of travelers' checks. That was all the money I had, and I needed to use it for food, gas, and lodging. In May of 1975, when I was 20 years old, gas was only .53 cents per gallon, so that wasn't a significant expense. I had no clue how much money a room would cost to rent for a night because I had never stayed in a motel before. Before leaving, I decided to check the *Bay City Times* and found an ad for a woman named Monica looking for another female rider to go with her to California and share expenses. I called her, and she was headed to Santa Monica. She wanted to take her car, which she'd purchased in Michigan, back to California. We met up to go over the details, and I agreed to drive my car, towing her car behind us.

Because money was tight, I vacated my apartment the week before the move and temporarily stayed with Hugh and his parents. The day before my move, I was excited and sad. I asked Hugh to help me load up my car, and he agreed. We packed up my 1968 Chevy Biscayne station wagon, and I put a sign in my rear window that read "LA or Bust!" – even though I was heading to Marcia's home in Riverside.

On the day of the move, I woke up to a quiet house since Hugh's parents were both at work, but they had left me a note wishing me well on my new journey and a Gemini pendant as a gift. Hugh and I put the last few items into my car, and we said our goodbyes. He gave me a hug and a kiss, and said, "I love you and don't want you to go." But his actions spoke louder than his words, and it was time for me to move on with my life. It was very painful and heart wrenching for me to leave, as I was heading to an unknown place almost 2,000 miles away. As I pulled away, I felt tears run down my face.

I headed to Monica's house to pick her up so we could begin our journey together. We made our way to the start of Route 66 in Chicago. When I saw the "Welcome to Illinois" sign, I was disappointed. I expected my surroundings to look completely different when I crossed the state lines, but it looked a lot like Michigan. It wasn't until we got to the Ozark Mountains in Missouri that the landscape took on a totally different view. There were small towns and cities that blended into one another across wooded, gently rolling hills and valleys. This was the very first time that I'd ever seen a mountain. While the view was incredible on the eyes, my car wasn't having it. My car was struggling to get down through the mountain roads with the extra weight of Monica's car. We pulled into the first gas station we saw in Missouri, and a kind man helped us to unhook the hitch and detach her car. She had to drive her car the rest of the way. After her first day of driving, her car had some issues that required a mechanic. Thankfully, it wasn't a major issue, and we were back on the road the next day. We caravanned for the remainder of the trip. Even though Route 66 passes by some amazing sites, I didn't pay much attention to my surroundings because I was so worried about losing sight of Monica and getting lost. We would drive from sunrise to sunset every day, stopping at night to get dinner and a room.

I became more excited the closer we got. I wanted to see the ocean, the mountains, and my friend, but most of all, I wanted to start a new life. On May 14, 1975, I reached my destination: Riverside, California. I called Marcia from a phone booth and she came to meet me, so I followed her to her house, where I met her husband Bob and their cats. I remember looking at the tall palm trees that were leaning against the blue California sky, and staring in awe at the San Bernardino Mountains. The sweet smell of the orange blossoms filled the air. I was really excited to start my new life in this beautiful place.

Living with Marcia was a fun experience. To start our day, we would get up in the morning and drink a lot of coffee. I was introduced to new hobbies, like macrame. Just 21 years old at the time, I'd never had any kind of hobby. We made 3 or 4 plant hangers and a few necklaces that I wore constantly.

One day shortly after I got to Marcia's, she wanted to take me to Newport Beach. It was crowded with all kinds of people. We took off our shoes and walked through the warm sand to the shoreline, where we cooled down with the cold, salty ocean water. When I looked out, there was no end to this magnificent body of water. It was the first time I ever saw the ocean. Huge waves were crashing on the shore with surfers riding in on them. My first thought was, "Wow, this is just like on TV." Lots of restaurants and small shops with beachwear and jewelry were within walking distance, too.

Now that I was starting to get used to the area, I needed to find a job. Marcia had a seasonal job as a produce sorter, choosing the oranges that were for juicing or for eating, so I got a job there as well. It was a fast-paced atmosphere; the fruit would come down on a conveyor belt, and I had to quickly decide which pile to put them in. Working there allowed me to save up money so that I could move out and get my own place. I moved out and shared a place with a roommate for a while.

I was excited about being in California, but I still missed Hugh. We stayed in touch regardless of our complicated relationship. Eventually he moved out to California and we got an apartment together. I bought a waterbed, which was the only piece of new furniture that I had.

Since I moved away from Riverside, I had to leave my job, so money was extremely tight. I found a job as a grocery bagger at the Pantry Market. I was glad it was within walking distance because I had no money for gas. Hugh would also have to donate blood as often as he could for money. Hugh eventually got work at a landscaping company and made good money. We were lucky Hugh's job paid him decently because my job at the market didn't last for very long. Several creditors from Michigan were calling me at work regarding unpaid bills that my ex-husband Don owed. The constant calls were too much for the Pantry Market; they got fed up and let me go. Now nobody, including me, was getting any money.

In January of 1976. Hugh and I were sitting at home, watching TV like any normal day. We had only been in this apartment for a short time and didn't know many people, except for a few of our neighbors, so, when I heard a knock on the door, I assumed it was a neighbor dropping by to say hello. To my surprise, when I had opened the door, it was a police officer.

"Are you Linda?" he asked.

"Yes."

"There's a family emergency. Call your sister Pam."

"Which family member is this about?"

"Your sister said your dad is in the hospital."

"Oh, okay. Thank you."

After the officer left, I called Pam. She had devastating news. Our dad had suffered from a brain aneurysm. By the time I called her, he had already undergone surgery to repair it, but the procedure left him in a vegetative state. Prior to the surgery, he told his doctor, "If I'm going to be a vegetable, I'd rather be dead." A few days after the surgery, he died. It was February 29th, 1976—a leap year. He was only 41 years old.

I had only been in California for nine months at this point, and I didn't have money to fly home. I borrowed some money for air fare from a friend of mine. It was my very first time on a plane. I was excited to have the experience of flying, but it was ruined by my reason for going back to Michigan.

My stepmother Sandy was so distraught that she didn't even attend the funeral. I went to visit her, but when I did, I found her lying on her back, unresponsively staring at the ceiling while her 5-year-old son, Kenny, drew on her face with red lipstick. Something was not right. She was taken to the hospital for a check-up and was diagnosed with schizophrenia. Sandy was then sent to an Adult Foster Care home and my Aunt Doris took in her three children. I returned to California less than a week later.

When I got back, Hugh and I were having problems. He'd always been a player, and there were a lot of beautiful women in So Cal and he wanted to play the field. I got sick of his back-and-forth attitude about our relationship, so I decided that I needed to move on and broke up with him again. I moved in with a friend I had met prior to Hugh's arrival. His name was Norman, and he was a nice-looking Italian guy with sparkling blue eyes, a full mustache, a light brown afro, and a beautiful California tan. Hugh sold my new waterbed before I had a chance to move it, so I took what possessions I had and left.

Chapter 4: No One Seems to Care, Including Me

Norman and I had fun together. He was on the rebound, and neither of us was looking for a monogamous relationship. Norman had been working as a machinist at Smith Tool, sheet metal factory. He didn't like the job very much, but he was making $4.03/hour when the minimum wage was $1.30, so it was a pretty good job to have. When he had vacation time, we went to Disneyland, took a road trip to Utah and Colorado, and even went to a nude beach in Deep Creek, California.

One night while I was living with Norman, I went out clubbing at this place in Newport Beach called "Jaws." I don't recall who I was with, but I do remember that when I walked out to the parking lot to my car, it was on fire, and smoke was coming out from underneath the hood. I ran back into the club and called the Fire Department. After they took care of the fire, a tow truck hauled my car to the junkyard. It was a total loss. I needed to figure out a way to make some money so I could get another car because it was pretty hard to have any type of job without transportation, especially in Southern California.

I talked to Norman about this to see what kind of suggestions he might have. To my surprise, he told me about a woman named Leta, who was a madam in need of some more girls. Norman knew about Leta because one of his coworkers was her neighbor. I was skeptical, but after giving it some thought, this job sounded like a quick, easy way to make money, so on May 12, 1976, I agreed to meet with Leta, and Norman gave me a ride. She was tall and had dark brown hair, and she seemed very nice. She told me that she thought I would do well and that men would find me attractive. I was a petite woman, at 5'2" and just over 100 pounds, with long brown hair and bright blue eyes. Despite the fact that I already had two babies, my body had bounced right back. Leta asked when I could start.

I explained to Leta what had happened to my car, so I wouldn't be able to drive to the man's house or motel room. The very next day, Leta wanted to set me up with a man. Norman worked second shift, so he wasn't going to be home until late in the evening. Arrangements were made for the man to come over to the apartment in Irvine. This was my very first time to have sex with a total stranger for money. I was wondering if the man would be overweight, unattractive, unclean, or have bad body odor. I was anticipating what I might see, feeling very anxious and a bit fearful. All at once, there was a knock at the door. I opened it and saw an average looking man. He introduced himself and I let him in. We immediately went back to the bedroom and had sex. It took about 10-15 minutes, and I was thinking that that was the easiest $50 I'd ever made. Within about a month, I'd made enough money to replace my car. I bought a 1971 VW Super Beetle, so I was able to get around and I wouldn't have to let strange men into my home anymore.

As I got to know the men better, they wanted to contact me directly without having to go through Leta. Obviously, since she originally introduced me to these regulars, she got a cut of my earnings even though my regulars thought that I should be able to keep all of the money. Eventually, I didn't want to have sex with any new men, and I just wanted to deal with the regulars that I knew and felt safer and more comfortable with. Ninety-nine percent of the men I saw were married and past their 40s. Most of them were business owners or were retired. Among my regulars, there are a few that I remember more than others:

First, there was a dentist. It wasn't until I met him in November 1976 that I got my teeth cleaned for the first time in my life. He also put in a bridge that I needed, pulled a baby tooth that I still had, and put braces on my top teeth. This would have cost a lot of money, but we just traded sex for dental work. We used to party in his office and get high on laughing gas. One time, he took me for a ride on his private plane. To me, he was a kind, generous man.

Second, there was a owner of a Mexican restaurant – my favorite food. He would get a motel room where we would meet; he was good for $100, and afterwards, I drove myself to his restaurant and he'd let me order anything that I wanted off the menu for free.

Third, the was a man who was single and younger than most who owned a carpet business. I'd go over to his place, drink some wine, and smoke some weed. He was a fun guy, always laughing. He introduced me to a couple with whom I became well-acquainted. There was an occasion where the four of us went to Mammoth, CA together. There were maybe one or two more couples on the trip, and they all rented a townhouse for the weekend. It was during this trip that I first put on a pair of snow skis and took lessons, which were a blast. I learned the wrong way to get off a ski lift really fast. Once, when I was skiing down the Hansel and Gretel hill, there was someone right in my path. They couldn't get out of the way fast enough, and I tripped over an instructor's skis and I fell. I got up and kept going, but that memory is very vivid in my mind. One of the evenings, everyone went out into the hot tub. It was a beautiful evening with the moon shining bright, stars everywhere. All the while, the hot tub was surrounded by snow. A few months after the trip, the man got into cocaine. I stopped seeing him because while he was high, he could have sex all night without climaxing, and I didn't want to deal with that. I figured he could call someone else. I found out later that his addiction got so bad that he compromised his carpet business.

The fourth man managed a place that sold new mobile homes. One time, he took me out to a really nice French restaurant in Huntington Beach. After our dinner was ordered, we were going to have a flaming dessert. The waiter unknowingly got some alcohol on his sleeve, and when he went to light the dessert, his whole sleeve was suddenly ablaze. He was okay, but it gave us all a scare. Another time, this man invited me to go to Florida with him. We flew down, checked into the motel room, and shortly after we got there, he got pulled out some cocaine (airport security was not like it is today). He started making lines on the table, and I wasn't happy at all; I'd wanted to go explore Florida. We could have snorted coke in a motel room in California.

Fifth, there was a jewelry maker who taught skeet shooting and hunter safety classes on the side. I took some gun safety and skeet shooting classes from him. He made me a silver ring with a mother of pearl set in it, and gave me a gold key charm on a necklace and a gold pen and pencil set. He would buy me Shalimar perfume, which was quite expensive, and lingerie, which I would wear for him.

Sixth, there was another man who bought clothing wholesale and sold it retail. We would meet at his warehouse and have sex there. As payment when we were done, he'd let me go through the dozens of racks of clothes and take whatever I wanted. The sheer amount of clothing available to me was overwhelming, and I'd go home after meeting with him with armfuls of brand-new outfits. I remember Norman being jealous because he'd go to work all week long for peanuts, and I was making out like a bandit. At least, I thought so at the time.

The last man I remember wasn't much of a regular, but he stood out to me. There was a day when I was driving down the 405 freeway and I saw a man driving a clean, shiny, silver, Rolls Royce. We came to a signal light and stopped. My windows were down and he was flirting with me. He asked me to pull over, so I did, and he asked for my phone number. I found him attractive, and he was clearly wealthy, so he was someone

I was interested seeing on a personal level. Unfortunately, after he called me, I found out he was married, so I saw him on a professional level. I don't recall what kind of business he owned or managed, but it was obviously very lucrative. If I was going to be a hooker, I was staying where the money was. On one occasion, I went over to his house, which was a massive, two-story place. We snorted some cocaine while I was there. In the 1970s, it was considered an insult if you turned down cocaine when it was offered to you. It was a rich man's drug.

There were occasions when I would only see a man once, and there were days when I was seeing more than one man per day. Since most of these men were well-off and living very comfortably, there were perks that I enjoyed in the beginning. I would be taken out to some very nice, expensive French, Italian, and Mexican restaurants – and yacht clubs. I enjoyed all of the great places in California. I was showered with expensive gifts. Since the loss of my two boys, I told myself I was going to try and enjoy life and make as much money as possible to get back on my feet. It was the seventies, and AIDs wasn't prevalent yet. I didn't always use protection, but I should have – I caught gonorrhea twice.

If I had to see more than one man per day, I would always take a shower in between dates. I would stand under the hot water for an excessive amount of time, trying to wash all of the residue from the previous man off of me before I moved onto the next. Even though I was lucky to have never come across an abusive man, I was still starting to feel used. While having sex with these men, my psyche would leave my body, and my body would feel like an empty shell, just an object for men. It was not fulfilling my emotional needs and it was damaging my mental health. An acquaintance of mine, Bonnie, who was also a hooker would occasionally come to parties with me. We knew we'd end up sleeping with someone by the end of the night, but we would just hope it wouldn't be someone disgusting or creepy. We could refuse if we wanted to, of course, but we wanted to make some money.

I didn't know until my late fifties that prostitution is a side effect of statutory rape, especially before the age of 16, which is the legal age of consent in Michigan. All these years, I didn't know that having sex at such a young age with someone who is legally an adult was considered rape because it had been consensual on my part with Don and Rich. However, under the age of 16, the human body is going through puberty and the brain is still developing, which means a young teenager is not old enough to make those kinds of decisions. I recently read that the most commonly cited reason for engaging in prostitution by rape survivors was that they were trying to regain some control over their lives and bodies: exchanging sex for money was seen as one way to control men's access to them. I never really looked at it that way until I read this, but it makes total sense, and I agree with this statement.

All in all, I worked as a hooker for about 18 months, which in hindsight was a relatively short time. However, it was long enough for me to realize that it was damaging my self-esteem and self-image and I needed to move on. While this job had fulfilled my material needs, I felt emotionally bankrupted.

Chapter 5: Looking to be Loved

In 1977, when I had some money for a change, I decided to take a modeling class through Ed Harrell Studio in Santa Ana, California. After hooking, my self-esteem and self-image were incredibly low, and I wanted to start practicing some self-care to improve those things. My instructor was very friendly, and she gave me a lot of great tips on improving my posture and my skin care routine. After this class, I pursued modeling for a while just for fun. One time I did a fashion show at the LA Convention Center. There were thousands of people in the crowd—I had never seen so many people gathered like that before. It was overwhelming. At first, I was scared, but after a couple of times walking out on the stage, I couldn't really see a specific face. There were so many. Then it became more fun, and I really enjoyed it. More importantly, it helped me see a different part of me outside of my damaged self-image. I gained confidence and it boosted my self-esteem. I felt like I was doing something positive and finally moving forward.

While I was working as a hooker, I met with a man named Paul a few times. Paul was living in an old house in a so-so neighborhood in Santa Ana. He worked at a printing company in Laguna Canyon at the time. He was tall and very slender, blonde-haired with blue eyes, a beard, and a moustache. He was divorced and lonely, but he seemed nice. After I met with him on a professional level a few times, he started to want to see me on a personal basis because he had come to like me. As I got to know him better, I realized that we both liked to bowl, see concerts, go camping, and go out to eat. He had two cats named Rum and Coke, and I loved animals so I enjoyed spending time at his place. He claimed that he was falling for me, and we started dating. We became more serious about the same time I stopped working as a hooker. By this time,

Norman and I needed our own space, so we went our separate ways and fell out of touch for a little while.

During the week of Thanksgiving Day in 1977, Paul and I went to spend the holiday with his family in San Francisco. During this visit, I went to see all the sights – Golden Gate Bridge, Lombard Street, Fisherman's Wharf, Ghirardelli Square – and also rode on a cable car. On Thanksgiving Day, I could smell the turkey cooking, the family was congregated and seemed to be enjoying one another's company. We were told the turkey was going to come out of the oven very soon. All at once, Paul asked me to go to the other room with him. He grabbed my hands and looked me in the eyes, and he asked me to marry him, and I said yes. He had proposed in the spirit of the holiday, so he didn't have a ring, but I didn't mind. Just like that, our day became more exciting, and we were both very happy as he shared the news with the family at the holiday dinner. They extended their congratulations and wished us both happiness. I knew that this was a hasty decision, but I was feeling very alone in a state across the country from my family. I missed having a familial relationship, something stronger and more permanent than just dating someone, and so I latched onto the life that Paul was offering me.

We drove to Clark County, Nevada, and got married in a little white chapel inside the Circus Circus casino on December 16, 1977. Paul bought me flowers that came displayed in a box. They were so beautiful and I was so happy and nervous that I forgot to take them out of the box before we got pictures taken. We went to dinner and played some slot machines. We were having a pretty good time until I got sick on a Quaalude I took. I usually liked those because they were very relaxing and fun, but it wasn't too fun to be sick on my wedding night. I got through it and we went back to So Cal the next day.

Even after getting married, Paul and I were still in our early twenties and felt very adventurous. We would occasionally have another woman over for a threesome. I experimented here and there, but I learned that I preferred men. Somehow, along the way, Paul and I got invited to an orgy in Hollywood. I'd heard about them going on but neither one of us had been to one before, so being curious, we agreed to go check it out.

The orgy was in a home at the top of a hilly street with a great view of the city. There were way more cars than we had expected. After we went in, we were shown around the place. There were rooms divided by sheets and curtains, and that was the only way anyone was able to have their own space. Even those spaces weren't private because people could still be seen and heard having sex. The house was packed with multiple couples who were having sex, socializing, eating food, and drinking alcohol. We participated to see if it would be something we'd want to do again or not, but I personally didn't feel comfortable with it. Even though I had hooked in the past, it was usually one-on-one. I felt that sex should be a private thing between two people. Paul saw some women he was interested in, but they weren't interested in him, and I was getting too many offers, so we decided to leave.

Not long after this experience, I found out that I was pregnant again. Paul and I weren't planning to start a family, and I didn't know for sure if he was the father. I was using birth control – a diaphragm, but apparently, there was a time I didn't have it positioned properly, resulting in my pregnancy. I should have insisted on the use of a condom to prevent pregnancy as well. At that time in my life, I was only 23 years old and I had lost custody of my two children. I wasn't ready to bring another child into the world when I was still getting to know my new husband. What if the marriage didn't work out? What if Paul found out the child wasn't his and didn't want to raise it? Because of the uncertainty and these concerns, especially after being at the orgy, I decided to have an abortion immediately after finding out I was pregnant. Even though I had the abortion as soon as possible, I still had a lot of feelings of guilt. I would sometimes think about whether that baby was a boy or a girl and what they would have been like. However, I still stand by my decision; I don't think I was at the right place in my life to be raising another child.

Since I wasn't working as a hooker anymore, I started working at a massage parlor – a legitimate facility, not meant for sex. I didn't mind the work, and I had to do something, plus I liked having my own money. I only worked there for a short time, however, because I had too many men asking me for sex while we were in the room. I didn't want to move backwards in my life, so I quit.

In the meantime, I was still living the lifestyle to which I had become accustomed. One thing that I was still doing was treating myself to a weekly manicure. As I got myself ready to go to my appointment, I looked at a beautiful ring that I had. It was one that I had made using the diamonds from the three rings that Hugh had given me and a ruby I had purchased. The four stones were set in a gold band. I didn't wear it all the time, but that morning my intuition told me to wear it, so I slipped it on before walking out the door.

Paul was at work and I was headed to Irvine for my manicure. I was gone for a few hours. When I got back, I could sense that something was wrong. Everything in the entryway and the living room looked fine, but when I walked into our bedroom, I immediately could see we had been broken into. Drawers were pulled open, and clothes were scattered all over the floor. I felt violated. It was an uncomfortable and creepy feeling to know some stranger touched our personal belongings, and it was scary to see how easily he got into the house, especially during broad daylight, not knowing if he was still in the house. I called my husband and the police. I was thankful that I went with my intuition and wore my ring. I don't recall anything being taken; we didn't have any cash hidden away. I decided to have a conversation with Paul because I had been wanting to move out of Santa Ana for a while.

Paul called Tarbell Realtors to list his house and show us some other homes. A week later, a bunch of cars pulled up and eight to ten agents went through the house rather quickly. They drove expensive cars and dressed really well, and when I saw this, my interest was immediately sparked. I watched them work to see what type of things their job entailed. At the time, it looked to me as if these people just had to look around our house for a few minutes and then call some buyers to see if they were interested. I knew at that moment that I wanted to look into a real estate career.

The Santa Ana house sold pretty quickly, and we found a new home in Mission Viejo. It was a planned community that was close to Paul's workplace, and everything was nice and new. I also really liked that location because it wasn't far from Laguna Beach.

I had been in California for 3 years, and it had been 5 years since I lost my boys. I had only had a little bit of contact with my mom during this time because I was still very hurt by her actions against me in court. However, shortly after Paul and I moved to Mission Viejo, she called and said she planned on moving to California, and she asked if she could stay with me for several weeks while she found a job, car, and apartment. I don't remember much about her stay with us, but eventually she got a job as a nurse's aide, moved out, met a man named Hutch who she started to date, and they lived together. They dated for several years and got married in 1985, and then moved to Nevada in 1987. I'd like to think that my mom missed me, but she never came right out and said that. More likely, she probably thought that if I could make it in California, she could too. She was tired of Michigan winters, so California seemed very appealing to her. Once she got on her feet and found a job, it was time to focus on myself and my own career goals.

After Paul and I got settled into the home in Mission Viejo (M.V.), I decided to look into getting my real estate license. While I was preparing myself to take the real estate exam, I got a job in new home sales. I thought it would be an ideal way to learn about new home sales versus getting into the resale market.

I was hired as a hostess by the M.V. Company in 1978 before I got my real estate license. I was working in the lower level of a custom home that was right on a man-made lake. At that time, the project was in the development stages and the lots were for sale to build on. For anyone to come in for information, they had to go through the guard gate up front. So anytime someone was on their way, I got a call. This was perfect for me. I was able to study during the downtime, and at lunch I would go out on the dock and enjoy the view of the lake and the Saddleback Mountains. I stayed at that location until all the lots were sold. Then, unfortunately, the home sold. I got moved into a single-wide trailer – a far cry from the beautiful custom home I used to work in – to work with a licensed real estate agent named Jeff.

One day I was sitting at my desk doing paperwork, and I looked up to see Jeff with his manhood in hand, masturbating in my face. I was in total shock, and I yelled, "What are you doing?!" I jumped up, grabbed my purse, and got out of there. I was extremely upset and discouraged that, after trying so hard to get out of the sex business and better myself, this situation happened in my place of employment. I started doubting whether or not I'd ever be free from being solicited for sex.

I drove straight home and told Paul. We decided I should report Jeff to the company's manager, and it was very embarrassing and an uncomfortable story to tell. They fired Jeff and gave me a few paid days off, but no other action was taken. I also decided to tell Jeff's wife about the incident so that she would know what kind of person her husband was, but she didn't seem too surprised, and I don't know if anything happened between them.

This incident motivated me even more to get my license. Paul and I both decided to study and take the real estate test at a location in San Diego. We took the test and waited three to four weeks before getting a letter in the mail saying whether we'd passed or not. One day we both got our letters; neither one of us passed. I only missed by 10 points – I was furious. I got another $10 money order that same day and sent in for another test date. In the meantime, I hit the books and studied some more. Paul, however, decided to give up after his first try. I was disappointed because I thought that this is something that we were going to do as a couple so that we would be able to support each other. Regardless of Paul's lack of motivation, I wanted to keep moving forward to better my life. In total, it took me three tries to pass the test, but I was determined to get my license. After I finally passed, I was elated! I felt such a sense of accomplishment because I had persevered and gotten something that I worked so hard for.

Now that I had passed the real estate licensing test, I was ready to get into the business and get myself some nice clothes and a new car. I went to Forest E. Olson, a Coldwell Banker company. I interviewed with a broker at the company, who was excited to hire me because of my enthusiasm and determination to make money for myself, which in turn made them money. Before I could start working for them, they required all new agents to participate in a Head Start Training Program. Every day for two weeks, I went to the class and learned everything I needed to know, from completing the forms to closing a sale. It was an excellent class. By October 1979, I was a licensed real estate agent.

There was an agent working in my office who I found very attractive. He had brown eyes, dark brown hair, and a mustache. We started spending time together – having lunch, previewing properties, and seeing each other in the office. I felt that I had more in common with this man than I did with my husband; he had a very professional air about him that Paul didn't, and he was already a part of the real estate business. Because we had been spending so much time together, he felt comfortable enough to invite me out after work one day to snort some cocaine, so we went back to his house in Laguna Canyon. Quickly, day turned into night, and we ended up doing more than coke. I didn't get home until the next morning.

In the meantime, my husband Paul was worried sick about me. I felt bad. He was really upset. I told him the truth because I knew he wouldn't fall for a lie. He said he wanted a divorce. I guess because of how we met, I thought it was no big deal, but it was to him. He filed for divorce on August 19, 1980.

Since we bought the house in Mission Viejo together, we both had money in it. He kept the house and took out a loan to pay me off. I got a $10,000 settlement and was out on my own again. I moved into a one-bedroom apartment in Laguna Hills. I felt remorseful about cheating on Paul, but I knew that what was done was done; I couldn't take it back.

After living on my own again, I got up one morning, opened my blinds, I saw another beautiful day. It appeared to be a perfect day to go to the beach. The beach is by far my "Happy Place." I decided I'd go to my very favorite beach— Laguna Beach. I had been feeling lonely and disappointed in myself since the divorce, and I wanted to take some time to reflect.

I had something to eat, put on my bathing suit, and threw on a pair of shorts with a sleeveless summer top. I grabbed my beach bag, which held my beach towel, Hawaiian Tropic suntan lotion, sunglasses, a cold bottle of water, and an apple for a snack until I got back home. I went out the door and got into my light tan, 1971 Super Beetle VW. It was a stick shift on the floor and a dream to park, and it was great on gas.

I headed down Pacific Coast Highway, also known as PCH. A scenic drive with palm trees on each side of the highway, PCH runs all the way up and down to all the coastal cities and all the beaches. I continued down the coast highway until I came to Main Street in Laguna Beach—the big shopping hub in the city. On Main Street, you can find a lot of beachwear, jewelry, and art shops, as well as great restaurants. The city doesn't allow any chain restaurants on this street, so every place is one of a kind. I oftentimes would go into the shops after I soaked up some of that California sun.

I turned off Main Street to find a place to park, and once I parked, I grabbed my beach bag and headed to the stairs that led down to the beach. Unlike Newport and Huntington Beach, which are completely flat, Laguna Beach has cliffs with multi-million-dollar homes that sit on the edge to get the best ocean view. It's a rather popular spot. On the weekends, there were usually people playing volleyball or hiking the trails on the hill above, and oftentimes, I'd see an artist out on the cliffs with their easel and paint brushes capturing the natural beauty.

As I went down the stairs, I enjoyed all the vegetation and the beautiful flowers that adorned the stairway from top to bottom. Once I got to the bottom of the stairs, I took off my sandals and sank my feet into the warm sand, feeling it squish up in between my toes. I'd find myself a spot and lay down my towel, looking forward to relaxing for a couple of hours. I didn't lay on my towel the whole time I was there, rather I would walk to the shoreline and explore some of the beautiful coves and huge rocks that lay along the shore. Of course, I looked for shells, too.

Once I had settled into my spot, I slipped off my shorts and tank top. I got out my coconut-scented Hawaiian tropic suntan lotion and lathered up—hoping to get the California tan I had always wanted. The temperature was perfect—mid to high 70's. Not scorching hot, but warm enough that going in the water feels refreshing. The sky was blue. The seagulls were flying overhead, just watching and waiting, hoping somebody would throw them some food. As I laid there, I noticed how peaceful it all was as I listened to the seagulls and the waves crashing into the shoreline.

When it was time to turn over and tan my other side, I decided to cool off a little first. I got up off my towel and walked over to the water. I gradually moved forward into the ocean, splashing a little water on my front side. It's hard to reach your own back, so I turned around and lifted my long, brown hair from my petite body, waiting for a wave to come and cool me off. I got cooled off, alright. The wave was so strong, it literally washed me ashore. I felt my legs scraping over the sand as the ocean showed me who was really in charge. It must have been quite a sight, but luckily, I was there on a weekday, so there weren't very many people there. I learned to never turn my back on the ocean.

After my day on the beach, it was time to get back to work. One day in May 1980, I was at my desk in the office of Forest E. Olson (F.E.O.)—which later was renamed to Coldwell Banker—making calls and doing paperwork. I had just received my first commission check for $1,500 after seven months of work, and I was excited that my life finally seemed to be moving forward. Suddenly, an agent from another office came in and invited me to a pyramid meeting that was going to take place later that evening. I didn't really know what it was all about, but I accepted the invitation. Later that evening, I went to the address of the house the agent had given me. There were nice cars parked everywhere, and the room was packed with people. Pretty soon the meeting began, a chart was displayed on an easel, and the concept of the pyramid was explained. People just needed to put in $1K, and the payoff for getting to the top was $16K. I gambled two thirds of my paycheck, but I worked hard to recruit people to keep my investment moving, and it paid off. I collected my $16K after one week. I was flooded with excitement and I wanted more, so I sponsored three people. The agreement was that if they made it to the top, we would split it 50/50. They all made it, making me $24K more. I took $5K from those winnings and bought in on a board with a $40K payoff, which I also ended up getting. My winnings totaled $80K, and I used this money to buy a 1979 white Cadillac El Dorado for about $11K. I loved that car. It was a beautiful luxury car with a red leather interior and all the bells and whistles. I also moved out of my apartment and put money down for a three-bedroom and two-bath home on Bent Tree Lane in Lake Forest, minutes away from my office. I thought I should invest some money in gold and silver, something I knew absolutely nothing about. I went to a place and bought a couple silver bars and some Krugerrands. I put the Krugerrands and silver into a safe deposit box at the bank with the rest of my money. Finally, I used some money to take a nice trip to the islands of Tahiti. After the vacation, I returned to California with lots of leftover winnings from the Pyramid, but I still went back to work right away.

This was one of the best moments in my life. I had gone through a lot to get to this point, but now I had a secure bank account, a career I loved, a nice car, a new home, and I was completely self-sufficient without needing to rely on anyone else.

Chapter 6: An Extremely Dangerous, Rotten Man

On December 31, 1980 – New Year's Eve – I was invited to a party in Newport Beach when I was 26 years-old, and I was dressed to the hilt. I wore a black silk jumpsuit, high-heeled shoes, and a beautiful white ostrich feather jacket. I was looking so good that even the women were coming by and rubbing their hands on my jacket. With that kind of attention, I was almost afraid of taking it off for fear that someone would steal it.

As the night went on, I met a very handsome man. He had dark brown hair, beautiful blue eyes, and a really nice beard and mustache. His name was Ray. After talking to him for a while, he pulled out a pretty full baggie of cocaine and offered to snort some with me. By the end of the night, we were wide awake and all tweaked up. The party was over and it was time for us to leave. I don't know how he had gotten to the party, but Ray did not have his own car, so we left together in my 1979 white Cadillac El Dorado and went to my home. When we were getting ready for bed, Ray showed me his one and only tattoo – a scorpion on the head of his penis.

Ray and I started dating and spending a lot of time together. We spent most of our time in my home in Lake Forest snorting coke. After it was gone, I was glad. I'd had my fill. The thought of anything going up my nose was no longer desirable. During this time, people at my real estate office were telling me that I was getting too thin. I had enough Pyramid money to pay my living expenses, so I eventually stopped showing up to work regularly. One day when I did show up, I was told to pack up my desk. I was mad at myself. I had worked really hard to have a real estate career, and it suddenly felt like I'd done it all for nothing.

Shortly after we started dating, Ray informed me that he was a Vietnam veteran (never in combat), an ex-police officer, and an ex-convict for getting caught with 500 pounds of marijuana. He also told me that he and his brother were going to Mexico to get some heroin. I'd never known anyone who used heroin before. Within the first couple of weeks, Ray got upset with me about something, so he grabbed me by the scruff of my neck and pushed me up against a closet door. He apologized right away, and I forgave him. After his trip to Mexico, he came back and persuaded me that if I sold my house and moved to Northern California with him, I could make a lot more money growing pot. I had just lost my real estate career, and I wasn't really tied to anything, so I agreed to do it. I had enough Pyramid money saved to cover our moving expenses. In March 1981, I sold my house and we moved into a U-shaped house in Willow Creek. The area was remote, perfect for growing pot.

We started the marijuana plants inside, and once they got big enough and it was warm enough, then we had to get them into the ground. The goal was June 1. We went out with our shovels and dug holes for the plants. We spread them out over the property. They got huge – probably eight feet – like small trees. They were beautiful plants. We had to tend to them daily. You had to be cautious of thieves, animals, and the law finding them. Keep in mind, this is the early eighties. The plants had to be watered and fertilized. The work involved a lot of mixing and hauling.

Finally, it was mid-September, harvest time. We had a lot of plants – I don't recall exactly how many. However, it equated to about 15 pounds of marijuana. We had some good skunk weed, sometimes referred to as night-time smoke. It's actually an Indica plant. We also had a daytime pot, or Sativa. After we dried, trimmed, and weighed up the pot, we decided to go to New York in November of 1982 to get rid of it. Ray knew somebody and made a call and they said they were interested. We were to bring all we had.

We drove from Willow Creek to Manhattan, New York, all the time knowing we were driving with all the pot in the car. We got there without any incidents, which was a relief. Once we arrived, Ray contacted his friend Randy. We had a trunkful of California bud to sell, and the east coast loves California pot.

Randy and three or four other guys met with us at a motel – either The Hotel Mayflower, across from the Park, or Gramercy Park Hotel. We stayed at both places. We showed them what we'd brought, and they really liked it. They decided to get five pounds from us, and at $2K per pound, that was $10K. I didn't feel as bad about all the sacrifices that I had made at that point. At some point, Ray must have left the room. I don't recall where he went, but the man who purchased the five pounds gave me the $10K, and I didn't mention this to Ray right away.

Later that night, Ray was drinking some wine and got pretty drunk. He started to get angry and violent, thinking that his friends never paid us for the five pounds of weed they had taken. One of his friend's girlfriends took a shaving cream can and smashed it against the side of Ray's head and face. Blood was everywhere. Ray ended up with a very black eye and a puffed-up cheek. I clarified to Ray that I had been given the $10K, and I was sorry for not telling him sooner. Every time I looked at his bruised face in the following days, I felt guilty. I was concerned his friends wouldn't do business with him anymore because of his behavior.

We stayed about one week during the Thanksgiving holiday in 1982. We were partying the whole time, riding in a limousine snorting coke, smoking weed, and drinking. For the holiday meal, we were invited to an Italian family's home in Peekskill, New York. They had a really nice dinner. The turkey was good but the mussels in marinara sauce were superb and something I'd never had for Thanksgiving before. We had a good time.

The Christmas holiday was just around the corner. We were done with business and it was time to go back to California. However, we left a whole trunk that resembled a treasure chest full of marijuana with Ray's friends to see if they could get rid of it. I wasn't crazy about the idea because I really didn't know these men. After a couple of weeks back in California, they called and told us they couldn't get rid of anymore – we'd have to come and get it. Ray and I talked it over and decided that I'd fly to New York by myself and pick up the trunk full of marijuana.

My flight to New York went just fine, and I stayed there for a few nights before I needed to catch my flight back to LA. The trunk of marijuana that I was supposed to be smuggling smelled really strong, so I bought dryer sheets and lined the trunk to disguise the smell. Luckily, they did the trick.

I got a ride to the airport and checked in the trunk and my suitcase. My blood pressure was through the roof, and my heart was racing with anticipation. Airport security in the 1980s wasn't even close to as intense as it is now. I was allowed to leave the trunk locked unless airport security suspected something. I had nothing else in the trunk but 40-gallon freezer Ziploc bags full of marijuana, equating 10 pounds. If they opened that trunk, I would have been arrested on the spot. And I didn't realize at the time that I was being used, as they now refer to it, as a "mule." I was definitely less suspicious-looking than a man with long hair, a beard, and a moustache.

The trunk was cleared without being opened. Everything was checked in, and I boarded the plane. The flight went well, but I was still on edge because of the huge amount of weed I had with me. My plane arrived at LAX and I still had to go down to the baggage claim area to get the trunk. Ray was there to pick me up. When the luggage started coming down the conveyor belt, we both stood there anxiously looking around, hearts racing, trying to look innocent, waiting for the moment that the trunk would appear so we could grab it and get out of there as quickly as possible. We did just that, and I finally was able to calm down and take a deep breath.

While we were getting our next crop started, Ray and I moved to a home in McKinleyville that met our needs. At this point, we only really had personal belongings. We were both a couple of gypsies and just did what we needed to do. I, at that time, was very adventurous. In some ways it was fun, but it was also very lonely. We didn't stay in one place long enough to make friends, and any company we had would be minimal.

We got settled in and got all of the plants started inside of the garage. Once the plants were about 9 inches tall, we still needed a place to finish growing them outdoors. Ray, the con man that he was, had a plan up his sleeve to find a place. He had no trouble going to a bar by himself, having some drinks, and meeting people. That's just what he did. It was like he was going out for prey.

One April night in 1983, Ray went out alone. Money was tight, but he said it was necessary to spend it socializing so we could find someone to rent us a new place to grow outside. He left about 10 pm – he figured by then, people had been drinking for a while and that would give him the advantage because, even though he was high on weed, he wasn't drunk. I was alone at home watching TV. Finally, I decided Ray was probably going to stay at the bar until closing, so I went to bed. Just past midnight, he came home – drunk already. He'd run out of money and had come back for the $20 or $30 we had at the time, which was all the money we had.

He asked me where it was and I lied – I told him I'd spent it on groceries. I didn't think he needed to drink anymore, or drive my truck back to the bar. My response made him furious. I was in bed, completely naked.

Ray immediately jumped on top of me and started to choke me, shouting and asking where the money was. His knees were pressed into my arms as I laid on my back with his hands around my neck. After a few terrifying moments, the world around me started to go black. Drunk as he was, he still somehow knew the limit and finally let go of my throat. As soon as I could, I got up. I grabbed my robe and put it on my trembling body. He continued to yell at me, but at that point, I knew I needed to get out of there.

As he pulled at my robe, we struggled as I approached the front door to leave. He was still fully dressed with his expensive, pointy-toed snakeskin cowboy boots on. When I was almost to the door, he pushed me down and kicked me with his boot extremely hard in my left thigh. Now I was even more terrified; he was out for blood. I wished I had just given him the money, but it was too late for that.

I finally managed to get out the front door and ran away as fast as I could. I had nothing – no shoes, no money, no purse or clothes. Only my robe – that was it. I didn't know any neighbors and it was past midnight. Everybody was probably either asleep or not home. I ran to the house closest to me to call 911 and get help, but my neighbors weren't home.

I was shaking like my body had never shaken before. Even though there was no one home, something told me to turn the doorknob, and it opened. As I walked into this quiet, dark house, I didn't know if somebody might get up and mistake me for a robber and possibly shoot me.

With that scary thought in mind, I called out as I walked in, "I'm your neighbor Linda and my boyfriend is trying to kill me – please help me!" Nobody came out or answered.

Pretty soon, I heard Ray outside calling my name. I didn't want him to know I was in there; I just wanted him to go home and sleep off his rage. Staying as quiet as possible, I hid behind a couch. After about five minutes, I didn't hear him anymore, but I didn't trust that he wasn't still out there lurking in the dark, hoping that I might come out. I stayed crouched down, waiting for the people to come home.

I don't have any clue how long I waited, but after what felt like an eternity, I heard voices and the door opening.

Again, I yelled out, "I'm your neighbor Linda and my boyfriend is trying to kill me – please help me!" and they did. My neighbors called a hotline for a women's shelter for me. The shelter sent two women out to pick me up. As soon as I saw the car that they said they'd be driving, I ran as fast as I could to get in and get out of there. My body was still shaking from fear, and I was cold. I was relieved, though, to have a safe place for the night. The shelter gave me some clothes and was very supportive.

However, because I had nothing and no money, I ended up going back home the next day. Ray apologized, just like he did the first time he abused me, and just figured that would be good enough and everything would go back to normal. I was beginning to see that I really didn't know Ray at all. In order to find out more about his abusive habits, I called his ex-wife, Lisa, the next day and asked if Ray had ever been abusive to her. She told me about the horrible black eye he had given her. Regardless of this new information, I had given up everything I had to be with Ray and to find profit in the marijuana we were growing together. I told myself that I needed to get something monetary out of this relationship before I left it.

Things got progressively worse after that terrifying night, though. Ray would seem amicable for a while, but he'd occasionally want to go pick up other women. Even though I never wanted to, he'd try to convince me to have a threesome with another woman, and if I didn't agree, he'd say he'd just sleep with another woman himself.

When money got really tight, he had met a couple of older men – probably in their sixties – who he pimped me out to for $50 each. So, maybe twice a month, I'd meet these two guys at this trailer and have sex with them. I felt cheap and dirty. Once I left, I'd go home and shower to get all the filth off. I felt the same way I had when I had been working as a hooker, and I'd stopped doing that for a reason.

I told Ray I didn't want to do it anymore, but he'd just yell and say, "How else are we supposed to get any money until our crop is ready?" Ray never worked when we weren't growing to try and make money; he just used me as his source of funds. I wasn't happy in this relationship at all anymore, but I was in so deep into the choices that I had made that I felt like I had to go forward with them.

Even though Ray and I moved around a lot, I still kept in contact with my sisters Pam and Deborah, and my brother Crockett through letters. My Aunt Doris was also keeping me up-to-date on what was happening with my ex-husband Don and my boys. She told me that Don was separated from his second wife, and the boys and their dad lived in the same trailer park as she did. My cousins would go over to their trailer and play. Aunt Doris said the place was dirty and the boys were being neglected due to Don's drinking. While Ray and I were living in McKinleyville, I decided to contact an attorney. It had been ten long, excruciating years since I'd seen my boys. There wasn't a day that went by that I didn't think about them. The toughest days were their birthdays and the holidays. I didn't even get to see Steve take his first step or hear his first words. I never saw them go to school. I was robbed of being a mother. When my rights were severed, in my mind I thought I'd just have to wait until the boys turned 18, when they were legally adults, so that they could see me if they wanted to. However, after hearing so many things from Aunt Doris, I couldn't wait any longer.

On April 21, 1983, I sent a letter to an attorney in Lakewood, someone that Ray had used before. I wrote down a list of questions that I had and enclosed some paperwork from the court's decision. The attorney called me back and told me that the decision was now null and void. I don't remember why because the words "null and void" were all that mattered to me. I was really excited and anxious to see and meet my boys again. I knew, however, that if I was by any chance going to be allowed to live with them again, I needed to finish what I was doing – making money from my marijuana – and get out of this horrible relationship with Ray.

It was November 1984. I called and got quotes on airfare back to Michigan and bought a ticket. I was going back home for the first time since May 1975. I was excited to reunite with my sons, my brothers, and my sisters.

Deborah came to pick me up from the airport in December 3, 1984. She kissed me on the lips and we hugged. She said she didn't realize how much she missed me until she saw me. In the nine years I'd been gone, a few nieces and nephews were born, and I hadn't met any of them yet. I made my rounds to see everybody and I took a lot of pictures.

My ex-husband Don used to work at the Knights of Columbus Hall, and he invited me to come by. I went there and sat down on a bar stool to talk with him as he continued to work. While we were talking, a teenage boy walked by me.

I thought it was just another employee that I didn't know, so I didn't say anything to him, nor did he say anything to me.

Don looked at me and said, "That was Daniel who just walked by."

My heart broke a little at those words; I hadn't even recognized my own son.

Don and I made plans to meet later on for dinner at a restaurant that his dad used to own.

Don had told the boys, "Get cleaned up and change your clothes – we're going out to dinner with your mom."

In their minds, they thought Don meant their stepmother, Wanda, until he told them I was their real mother. It wasn't until then that Steve found out that his stepmother wasn't his real mother. Daniel did have some memory of me with my long brown hair, but he still didn't know me.

When I saw them, I wanted to hug them and never let go. I did hug them, but I didn't want to overdo it because as far as they were concerned, this was the first time they had really met me. We talked as we ate our meal and tried to keep the conversation light. I asked them how school was, what kind of classes they liked, and how their grades were. Daniel told me that he was taking guitar lessons. I was happy to find out as much as I could about their interests and personalities. I couldn't stop looking at them. I was overwhelmed in every way.

One evening during my eight-day visit, Don came over by himself to my motel room. We reminisced and ended up having sex. My time with Don was like déjà vu. He was the first man I had ever been intimate with, so that will always be a special memory for me. One evening, the boys, Don, and I went to the Knights of Columbus Hall where we ate and danced together. I later found out that the boys were hopeful that maybe we would get back together. It turned out that Don was hopeful too; he told me that he still loved me and asked me to marry him again. I did care for Don; he was the father of both of my boys. However, I was not in love with him. I guess I gave him the wrong impression when we had sex. I told him that I didn't want to marry him and clarified that all the pain and suffering I went through would have all been for nothing if we got back together. Don understood but was disappointed.

The eight days went by too quickly, but I had spent as much time as possible with my boys. During this time, they had bought me two blown glass pieces: one was a harp and the other was a heart with a bird on it and a small hanging pail. They were beautiful and very fragile, and I treasured them. Before I knew it, my visit was over and I needed to head back to California. It had felt wonderful to be out of Ray's clutches, but I knew I was going to return to him. It was clearer than ever in that moment that I needed to leave him. When it came time to say my goodbyes to my boys, it was incredibly difficult. I did my best to hold back my tears. I went outside and waited to board the plane. Once I walked up the staircase and got to my window seat, I looked out and saw Don, Daniel, and Steve all standing on the pavement, waving to me. We waved and waved until the plane departed and we couldn't see each other anymore. Tears were running down both my cheeks, and I cried on and off most of the way home.

Don didn't want to give up on my so easily, so he sent me a couple of love letters in the mail when I was back in California. He told me that the other women he's had in his life hadn't meant anything to him like I had. He also said he would love me till the day he died. I turned him down again in my replies, but I still have those two letters.

Once I was back in California, reality set in again, and I went back to my life with Ray and our marijuana plants. Since money was always tight while I was with Ray, everything that I'd bought with the pyramid money had been sold. I wasn't happy that I was foolish enough to let him manipulate me into this situation. The only thing I could do was move forward.

When I got back home to McKinleyville, our plants were getting to the point where they were ready to go into the ground. Somehow Ray found a couple that owned a piece of property in Weitchpec on an Indian Reservation near Hoopa.

The four months we spent growing outdoors in Weitchpec in the summer of 1985 was like one long camping trip. Our home was just an A-frame structure that was only a shell without any insulation, electricity, or running water. We didn't have any appliances, so we would use my two-burner camping stove to cook, and I had to get blocks of ice to keep our food cold. In order to bathe, we hoisted a camping shower up the tree in the early morning to let the water get warmed by the sun as much as possible. A lot of times, even in the late afternoon, the water was cold enough that I would let out a scream.

When the plants we had indoors were big enough to move outside, we had to plant them in big black plastic bags because we were in the mountains and there was more rock than dirt, so they couldn't go into the ground. We spread our crop out all over the property. It was a fulltime job and a lot of manual labor – more work than a person would think unless they'd done it before. The closer it got to harvest time, the more stressful things got. There was always fear of the plants getting stolen, getting busted, or the plants getting damaged by animals or a heavy rain.

Every once in a while, Ray would offer to go to town to run some errands. Naturally when he'd go, he'd find the only local bar in town. One time he went alone and came back drunk. I was really upset that he'd spent our only money on drinks for himself rather than on our basic needs. I was yelling at him at the top of my lungs because I was so angry. Of course, he wasn't worried that anyone could hear me. There wasn't anyone close by. I don't know how we got money to get out of that mess, but Ray knew I was resourceful and would figure something out. I've been a fixer and survivor all my life, but it was getting really old. I was tired of being the one to take on all the responsibility.

Everything was cut down and drying in the small A-frame structure because there was no place else that we could safely dry. Once some of it was dried, manicured, and bagged, it was ready to sell. Before heading to the city, we needed to meet up with the couple to pay them for letting us grow on their property. We were to give them a set amount of the yield, and Ray had given the owners a wedding ring set of mine for collateral until our debt was satisfied. Once we were ready to leave, Ray gave them a partial payment and I never saw my rings again. He didn't care – Ray was about Ray. Because Ray ripped off that couple, we left abruptly. We moved out of Weitchpec to Mira Monte, near Fresno, to finish drying and manicuring our product to get ready to sell.

One day, I got a call from the police telling me that they had my oldest son Daniel with them in Lakewood, California. He had been arrested for stealing a car, but since he was only 15, they would release him to my custody. I drove down to get him and asked him how he had gotten there. He told me that he and a friend had stolen a car and $200 from a print shop and driven from Bay City, Michigan to Lakewood, California to see me. Daniel didn't know where I was living nor what I was doing, so he had gone to Ray's parents' house – the only address he had for me – and the police had found him there.

This wasn't the most opportune time to take in my son. Of course, I wanted to have him with me, but I was in a very abusive relationship and Ray and I were doing illegal things.

I didn't want Daniel to get involved. Ray wouldn't have been a good role model or father figure for him. After driving him back to Mira Monte and letting him stay for a couple of days, I had to send him back to Michigan. It broke my heart.

After Daniel left, Ray and I planned on going to the city to sell our crop. I needed my hair trimmed before we left because it was quite long, well past my shoulders. Money was tight, so Ray said he could trim it for me. I sat on a chair with my back to him and he started to trim my hair. We were in an area of the kitchen and I wasn't looking in a mirror. By the time I was able to see all the hair on the floor, it was too late. He'd cut off all my beautiful long hair. When he was done, it barely came past the natural hairline at the back of my neck. I was extremely upset. I'd trusted him to just trim my hair. All I could do was cry.

Regardless of this new incident of emotional abuse, Ray and I still moved further south and stayed at a motel in Newport Beach while looking for an apartment. I recall sitting on the chair in the room, and suddenly Ray went into a rage about something. It could have been about anything or nothing at all, but I think he was just looking for an excuse to drink along with his smoking weed. Suddenly, out of nowhere he slapped me alongside my head with his hand cupping my ear. My ear was ringing and it ached terribly. Then, after the slap, he threw a cold drink directly in my face. I don't remember what it was, but it was sticky. I'd never felt so humiliated in my whole life. The abuse was getting worse and his temper was getting shorter. I knew I had to get away from him.

We rented an apartment in Newport Beach, but the biggest concern on my mind was, we're in the city and close to the bars, which Ray was already contemplating beforehand. As usual, we were doing okay until he got the urge to go out and tie one on. Even though the drinking wasn't daily, when Ray did drink, he drank to get drunk. Beer was one thing – whiskey was a whole other story. In my experience, whiskey makes men mean and demeaning. I used to think it was the alcohol that made him abuse me, but I know now that was just the excuse that he gave to justify his behavior. He knew what he was doing.

It was a sunny Southern California afternoon, and I was home alone doing some cleaning while Ray went out for a while. I don't recall where he had been, but when he returned, he told me that he wanted to have sex. I said no. He decided that he wasn't going to take no for an answer, he pushed me into the bedroom, and forced me down onto the bed. He got over me, and put his arm across my neck and shoulders, holding me down while he pulled my shorts and panties down and raped me. I recall, when it was over, I was furious. I asked him, "Why did you do that?" He just ignored me like it was no big deal. I knew that if I had called the police at that time to tell them what happened, they would have just said, "Well, he's your boyfriend," and wouldn't take me seriously. This guy was a dangerous animal, and I was afraid of him. Somehow, someway, I needed to break this relationship off, but I still needed money and a plan.

Once it was time to start growing again, we moved to Eureka. We didn't make profit on the first two crops, but I was holding out hope that this third crop would make me some money so I could get out of this relationship. We stayed with a couple, Renee and Howard, while we got our plants started indoors. I got a job at a Greek restaurant to support Ray and myself. Ray, as usual, just relied on my income. Even though I wanted to wait for a return on my investment, I got sick of it. It got harder and harder to give myself excuses to stay with Ray. I was talking to my friend Norman who was living in Livermore, not far from San Francisco. He told me that he never liked Ray, and when I told him about the abuse, he said I could come there and stay with him. I had to call my workplace and tell them I quit. I felt bad because I always gave notice when leaving a job. Once that was settled, I got some stuff together and when the opportunity presented itself, I hit the road. I got to Livermore and stayed with Norman for a few days.

When I left, I didn't take my two cats with me. I felt really bad leaving them behind, but I wanted to get away from Ray. I hoped he would be decent enough to take care of them. After a couple of days, I talked to Renee and she said Ray wasn't taking care of the cats and they were being left outside to fend for themselves. I was really upset, so I left Norman's house and went back to Eureka. I'm sure the story about my cats was Ray's idea and Renee was in on it. He figured that would get me back, and it did.

When I got into town, there was a phone booth in front of a Denny's restaurant and I called Norman to let him know I was back in Eureka. Before I was done with my call, I turned around and Ray was standing right there. He scared me so much that I jumped. I don't know how he found me in the phone booth, but I guessed it was his police training at work. Although I was back in Ray's clutches now, I knew I would get away from this man, eventually.

Ray made some kind of a deal with a guy in McCann, in Mendocino County, which is part of the triangle – Mendocino, Trinity, and Humboldt Counties. The property was about 100 acres. There was hay on the property, and the acreage also had a river, the Big River, running alongside it. On the other side of the private property, there was land that belonged to the Louisiana Pacific Co.

This property had a small house on it – better than the A-frame that we'd been in previously. It had electricity and running water at least. We got settled in and got the ground ready for the plants. Ray found an area and we cleared the debris away. The great majority of the plants went there and about four of them were just to the right of the house. We didn't plan on having any visitors, so I guess Ray thought it would be okay.

It was the last week of July, and Ray and I were constantly caring for our 300 plants. We both needed to get out because we had cabin fever, so we went into the town of Garberville and had something to eat, then went to a bar afterward. We met a woman at the bar, and Ray explained to her that we were getting ready to harvest our crop and asked if she would be willing to help out, so she came back with us. The next morning was particularly hot, and not long after being in the garden, I took off my jeans, top, and sweatshirt, so I was down to tennis shoes and underwear. Ray just had on a pair of shorts, shoes, and a straw cowboy hat. He always took our rifle with him into the garden while we worked, and we had a Pitbull, Bud, and a black cat, who were both in the house that morning.

All of a sudden, out of nowhere we heard a voice and looked up to see six deputies from the Eureka Sheriff's Department accompanied by two Department of Fish and Game officers. My heart was racing and my adrenaline was through the roof.

In the moment, I thought to myself, "Oh my God, are we going to be shot and killed or just arrested?" They saw the rifle that was lying by the garden, and they saw that we were not only unarmed, but also barely clothed. They allowed me to get dressed before the camera crew from the Hollywood-based channel KHJ-TV started to record the whole event. Because of the amount and quality of the plants, they thought this had been a huge operation run by 10-15 people, but it was just the two of us. They escorted us out of the garden and arrested us.

We later were told that while we had been at the bar the night before, a man from the Fish and Game Department trespassed onto our private property. He claimed that he had been investigating poachers on the Louisiana Pacific Co. property, and that he saw the plants closest to our house and reported his findings to the Eureka Sheriff's Department. I knew he was lying because he would have had to walk to our house on foot since we had a long steel bar with a lock on it that ran across the driveway. He wouldn't have been able to drive in any other way.

We were escorted up to the house with guns pointed at us, and our dog was secured. They searched our house and took things like our triple beam scale, any paraphernalia, the rifle, a nice nickel-plated 9 mm handgun that Ray had talked me into buying, and anything else related to our marijuana.

We were asked if anybody else lived there, and we told them no, but the woman we had brought home from the bar was still sleeping in the back of the pickup truck. Before she even got to see the plants, one of the deputies knocked on the door of the truck and said, "This is the police, get dressed and come out." They questioned her and then told her she could go.

After she left, the two of us got into the back of the police car. Our hands were in cuffs and we were now heading to Eureka County Jail, where we were booked and locked up. Within a few hours, we got out on our own recognizance by signing our names to agree to show up for court.

When we returned back to the property, and went to look at our once-beautiful garden. All of our plants had been cut down and hauled away. It was very depressing, and I felt like I was going to throw up. All of our hard work had gone down the drain, and all that I'd gone through with Ray and the assets I once had were history. All I had was a dog, a cat, and an abusive boyfriend. There wasn't anything left to smoke – and if we had any, they would have taken it.

There was only one thing left to do: drown our sorrows in alcohol. We went to Garberville to the local bar. Ray got drunk very quickly, but I only got a little buzz going. We were both extremely angry and devastated. When it was time to go home and figure out what to do next, I was uncomfortable leaving with Ray – he was a time bomb waiting to explode. We went to the truck and I told him that I should drive since he was drunk. He got into the driver's seat and demanded I get in. I wouldn't. I ran down the road and he followed me, trying to coax me into the truck. I was feeling scared now – I didn't want to ride with him. As he continued to drive and I kept refusing, he double parked the truck and came running toward me. I didn't know what to do but I just knew, deep down, that I shouldn't get close to him.

I came upon a restaurant that I'd never set foot in before. I ran through the front door at lightning speed, into the kitchen, and said, "My boyfriend is after me and I'm afraid he's going to kill me." Sure enough, he followed me into the restaurant saying he just wanted to talk to me. Once again, the glib talker he was, I left with him against my intuition, and he drove us home.

Now it was dusk. We arrived at our front gate, where the lock had been cut, so we just drove right through. Up until now Ray had been quiet, but once we got to that point, he started yelling at me, blaming me because we left the day prior to get out for a while. As he was still driving, he went into a rage. He reached over, pulled the handle of my door to open it, and pushed me out while the truck was still moving. I was running alongside the truck because he had me by my head of hair, dragging me along. I should have listened to my gut. At least I didn't need to worry about him shooting me because our guns had been confiscated, but he could still beat me or just let me go then run me over.

Ray finally stopped the truck and I got back in. We got back to the house and tended to the cat and dog. I was still trembling with fear. I didn't want to spend the night with him. There was absolutely nobody close by who I could go to for help. The only way out of there was to drive to civilization.

Completely out of options, I decided I would drug him with some Unisom. We had sloppy joes that night for dinner. I ground up three or four Unisom and sprinkled it in the sloppy joe meat. He definitely got tired. Pretty soon he went to bed. Well, that was my chance to get away. Problem was, if we had any money left, it wasn't much. We had just gone out to the bar, and I didn't know where I was going to go if I left. I was too scared to leave. I felt like I knew I would have to deal with him again after I left, and it just might make things worse. The only way I could see to get out of this abusive relationship was to relocate to So Cal, to the city. I needed to get back around people I knew and could help me get out alive.

Ray woke up the next morning none the wiser to my second attempt to leave him for good. With no crop, no money, and a court hearing coming up, we knew it was time to leave that house. We informed the guy whose property we were using about the bust and let him know he wasn't going to be getting anything. I never liked Ray making empty promises with people we rented from, but in this case, we really had nothing left to give.

After we got busted, we moved back to Long Beach. I knew for certain that I didn't want to grow anymore and I needed to get away from Ray for good. I just wanted to close that chapter of my life and start fresh, but I needed to figure out how. Since all of the weed we had grown was taken away from us, Ray would get ahold of a pound of pot and sell it in smaller amounts for a profit. He was always hustling illegally. He could look you straight in the eyes and tell you the biggest, fattest lies his brain could come up with. Soon, I thought he would start to believe them himself.

We lived just one street over from Ocean Blvd. and the Pacific Ocean. There was clean air there, and I liked to run on the sandy beach from the steps of the lifeguard tower and back. I'd spend as much time at the beach as I could. One day, Ray and I were taking in some sun. I got up to use the bathroom, and when I returned, Ray suddenly decided to go back to the apartment, but I wanted to stay and tan for a while. He gathered his stuff and headed to the stairs. Within five minutes after Ray left, I felt a tap on my right shoulder and a man's voice asked me to roll over. When I rolled over, I saw Ray standing at the top of the hill, watching me while holding onto the railing. Immediately, the man leaned down and planted a very nice, soft, warm kiss on my lips without hesitation. I'm sure I displayed a very dumbfounded look on my face. He told me how beautiful he thought I was and how much he desired me. The man was attractive, and I was flattered by the compliment and he seemed very sincere. He said his apartment was close by, so I picked up my towel and we walked there, had sex, and I left. For the first time in a long time, sex was actually enjoyable. While I was walking home, I realized that he never asked for my phone number, which was kind of surprising because of his earlier behavior, but I didn't think about it too much at that time. I was afraid because I knew Ray had seen the guy kissing me, but strangely, he never said anything. It became clear to me at that moment that Ray had probably pimped me out to that man while I was in the bathroom. Within a few minutes, I took a shower to get the sand, suntan lotion, and mostly the smell of lust off of me. Knowing what Ray had probably done, I felt disgust in his actions. I never saw that man again.

The next day, Ray told me he needed to use my car, so I thought I would go grocery shopping early so he could use the car when he needed. We were in an upstairs apartment, and when I got home, I had a grocery bag in each arm. I knocked on the door with my arms full and Ray opened the door to let me in. After I got in, he shut the door, turned around, and sucker punched me right in my stomach with his fist so hard that it knocked the wind out of me, and I fell to my knees and dropped both bags on the floor. I didn't know what his problem was this time; it could have been anything. Either way, he was sick and I'd had enough of his abuse.

While we were in the city, I did some telemarketing for Narconon which I enjoyed quite a bit; I made some pretty good sales. This was Ray's way of trying to make it look like we weren't smoking or selling marijuana while he was waiting for his court date. During one of the events that Narconon hosted on May 4, 1986, I was able to get out of the house long enough to look at some apartments without Ray knowing. I had some money saved up from my part-time job, and needed to be in charge of my own life again. I found a place that was in a safe area that I could afford, so I put a deposit on it.

I knew Ray would be angry when he found out I was moving, but I wasn't going to let that stop me. However, after I naively told him where my new apartment was, Ray drove by the place. After he saw it, he told me how much of a dump it was. I didn't expect him to say anything good about it, seeing as I was going to leave him, but he sweet-talked me one more time, and I didn't go through with my move. I lost my deposit on the apartment. I was angry with myself for not leaving. However, I began to realize which of my plans hadn't worked, so I needed to try something different. I knew I needed money – bigger than peanuts – and once I got away from him this time, I wasn't going back.

Fortunately, I'd taken my continuing education and kept my real estate license intact. I really enjoyed the short time I'd spent in real estate when I was in the Saddleback Valley F.E.O. office. Now I was in Long Beach, and there was a Coldwell Banker office right on Pacific Coast Highway. I really liked C.B. They've been around for a long time, and I felt since I was just getting back into the business again, this would be the place to be. Feeling confident, I made an appointment with the broker and she welcomed me to the office. I had my own desk and my Buick Riviera. I really liked the location of the office, and even though Long Beach was a challenging market, I rose to the challenge and was successful.

I got to know my coworkers. There was one agent in particular named Robert. He had black hair with a receding hair line, brown eyes, and a very heavy beard. His two top front teeth overlapped slightly, showing when he smiled and laughed. He was a shorter guy—about 5' 8" and 155 lbs.— but very knowledgeable and a hard worker. He was born and raised in Long Beach and knew the area quite well. We became friends and he made it clear that he wanted to date me. Eventually, his persistence wore me down, but most of the time Robert and I spent together was at work.

Robert had been a real estate agent for a while, and he decided to invest in his own real estate. He started by purchasing a few units in an apartment building at 8th and Pacific in Long Beach. The building had a security door that served as the main entrance. Robert told me his building had a vacancy, and I saw this as an opportunity to get away from Ray. I told Robert about Ray's abuse, and he was more than happy to help me. He offered an apartment to me, but he really was offering me safety and independence, which I was very excited to have for the first time in years.

I was waiting for the opportunity to leave without Ray's knowledge. I learned my lesson from last time; I was keeping my new apartment a secret. Ray and I needed money, and the only way Ray knew how to get money was selling weed. When he told me that he was going to take a trip up north to get rid of an ounce and get some more marijuana, I was thrilled at the perfect timing. I told Robert and asked him to help me move while Ray was gone.

When Robert showed up, I had my stuff packed and ready to go – photo albums, clothing, personal hygiene items, my 33's, bedding, and my cassette tapes. It wasn't much, but it was all I really cared about. As we continued to go back and forth between the cars and my second-story apartment, my adrenaline was pumping. I was excited to have a safe place to live, but nervousness lingered. What if Ray came home early? Luckily, that didn't happen. The last box was in Robert's car, and relief washed over me. A weight had been lifted. I was leaving for good.

We unpacked the cars, and I settled into my apartment. Robert provided a bed for me, but otherwise, I had no furniture. Now that I had moved out, I knew I'd have to be strong and stick to my guns when Ray got back. I was really afraid of what he might do, but I finally figured out that I couldn't fall prey to his threats anymore or our relationship would never end.

Ray finally returned home to a half-empty apartment. He was livid, I'm sure, but he didn't know where I'd moved to, so he didn't come after me right away. A few days passed, and I was about to go inside my apartment building, but before I had unlocked the security door, I heard Ray's voice from behind me. I turned around, and there he was. He knew where I worked, so he must have followed me home from the office. Trying to charm me, he nicely asked why I moved and claimed that he just wanted to talk. Clearly, he was interested in getting into my apartment either to beat me or convince me to move back in with him. Either way, I wasn't falling for that anymore. I was scared, but I was strong enough to refuse him. I ran to my car that was parked on the street, locked the doors, and waited for him to leave. Still maintaining his nice demeanor, he tried to talk to me through the car window. I told him to go away a few times, but I soon stopped responding. Eventually, he gave up and went away, but his attempts to get me weren't over.

The next day, he called me on my new phone number, and I assumed he got it from the real estate office. He'd call and call until I answered, and I'd just hang up on him. There was no caller ID then, and I didn't want to miss any calls from clients. I answered each call but immediately hung up when I heard his voice. Then he'd call back to hang up on me. It was all about power and control for him, but I was taking it back. He threatened to tell my broker that I'd been growing marijuana in Northern California. I said, "Go ahead, I don't care what you do or say – I'm not coming back." After weeks of harassment, he told me that he'd stop if I gave him my car. I didn't want any more trouble from this guy, so I decided to give up my car in exchange for freedom from him for good. This successfully ended the relationship, and just in case he did come to my office, I informed my broker about the abusive relationship I was getting out of. I even told her to call the police on my behalf if he showed up at the office, which fortunately wasn't an issue.

After a couple of months, Ray stopped calling. I finally had my free will back; there was no more controlling, physical abuse, or humiliation. The sense of relief was so intense that it's hard to describe. It was as if I took a deep breath and, while exhaling, the prison walls around me came down. I felt free as a bird. Now, I was able to continue on with the real estate career I loved so much.

Chapter 7: One Night on Broadway

Because of my enthusiasm for the great market conditions, I was busy at work and creating a lot of success. One day, my broker asked me to come back to the lunch room with her to look at the Sales Board. Here, any agents who took a listing or made a sale recorded it on this board for everyone to see. She pointed out that I did 26% of that month's office business. I was so busy I didn't bother to compare my sales to others, but I was pretty proud of myself, especially seeing how I didn't know the area and was dealing with the ending of an abusive relationship. I was presented with a Bronze Award for earning over $30,000 that year, 1987.

In addition to my success at listings and sales, I was a closer when it came to floor time. Floor time is when you answer the phone for a two to three-hour shift, hoping to arrange to meet with prospective buyers or sellers. I loved floor time. I knew the right questions to ask to understand how motivated the person was to buy or sell, and if the person was hot, I got them in the office immediately. I was so good at floor time that I helped model for trainees. So, when I got an opportunity to cover someone's floor time shift, I eagerly took it. During the shift I was covering, I took a call from a seller who wanted to list "The Galaxy Towers Penthouse," right across the street from the ocean with amazing views. I set up an appointment and got the listing. After seeing the property, I felt incredibly lucky. It was a beautiful place. It was an expensive purchase for someone, which meant a big listing commission for me. I listed it for $350,000. The penthouse sold, and I closed.

After the penthouse closed, Robert came across a 1982 Mercedes Benz (MBZ) 240D parked in Seal Beach and told me about it. We went to see it, and I took it for a test drive. It was a four-year-old car with 47K original miles. It was white with a palomino-colored leather interior, and it had a sun roof. The ashtrays had never been used and the back doors were still tight. I used my nice commission for a down payment on it, and I was really excited when I drove it home.

With my life seemingly back on track – a new car, a successful career, and a safe home – I was able to focus on my relationship with Robert. Now that Ray was completely out of the picture, we were free to date openly. Robert was very frugal, so he knew of multiple restaurants with specials for each night of the week, and he only wanted to go to those places. One time, when we were planning to go out to eat, he was telling me about a particular restaurant.

"It's a nice restaurant. The food is good. Very reasonable prices," he told me, full of pride as he was always looking for a good deal.

I looked him straight in the eyes and said, "Robert, I want to go to an unreasonable restaurant." We both busted out laughing. Instead of going to his reasonable restaurant, he took me out to a fancy, expensive steakhouse in Newport Beach with white table cloths and cloth napkins.

After spending more time with him, I thought I wanted a committed relationship with Robert. We had a lot of fun together and had been seeing each other exclusively. I thought we were on the same page, but he wasn't sure what he wanted. After having an in-depth conversation with Robert, he concluded that he did not want to commit to me, which was shocking and upsetting. I was heartbroken, but even though our romantic relationship didn't work out, we maintained our friendship.

One day I was in the real estate office, and an agent said I had a phone call. I picked up the phone, and it was my ex-in-laws from Michigan telling me that my ex-husband, Don, was in prison again and they were getting too old to raise my boys themselves. The boys wanted to come to California and live with me.

The day that I'd been waiting for had finally come. I was going to be a mother – at least try to be. There were many things I needed to do to prepare, but I only had three weeks until Daniel arrived. The first thing I needed to do was get clean. I'd been using marijuana on and off for years, and I thought quitting was an important step if I was going to be a good role model. I went to the phone book and located the phone number for Narcotics Anonymous (NA). I started attending meetings immediately. I knew I needed to be going for myself, but my boys coming back gave me the incentive.

In early 1988, my oldest son Daniel arrived in California. He was 18 years old. Daniel was 5' 9" and thin—only 150 pounds. He wore black-rimmed glasses and a gold chain necklace that he got from his father. Much like his father, he had a laugh in every conversation and was outgoing. Daniel was hopeful for this new chapter of his life, since his childhood was certainly filled with issues. He was separated from me when he was three and a half years old. He lived with eight other kids, an abusive step-mother, and an alcoholic father. He also had spent time in Adrian Juvenile Facility. Moving to California gave him the opportunity to start fresh, and he was excited to leave the past behind.

Steve came a little later on in June of 1988. It was the end of the school year, so he had stayed in Michigan to finish his freshman year. He was only 15 at the time. Unlike Daniel, Steve wasn't as excited about the move. He really didn't know me at all, so he felt like he was moving in with a stranger. He was excited to be in California, of course, because of the sun and surf, but it was a significant transition for him to live with a mother he didn't know he had until he was 12 years old.

Now, after all these years, I was reunited with my two boys. Even though I was really hopeful and excited, I was anxious, too. I didn't know how to parent two teenaged boys that I hardly knew. I figured strict ground rules were a good place to start. I gave them curfews. No friends were allowed over while I was at work. My most important rule was no drugs. The boys knew that I was going to NA to stay clean and that no drugs would be allowed in the house. I made it clear right away that they would be kicked out if they broke this rule. I didn't want them ending up like their father; they needed to go to school and make something of themselves.

Having my boys with me once again meant the world to me. I carried a void deep in my heart for many years. However, after just a short time of being together, I realized just how unprepared I was to parent them. When Daniel was 18, I was only 33. So, when Daniel told his friends that I was his mother, they didn't believe him. Often times, when the three of us went places together, people would think Daniel and I were a couple, which revealed just how young I was when he was born.

As time went by, it became very apparent to me that Daniel had a lot of anger and rage towards me. His go-to excuse for bad behavior was "If you and Dad wouldn't have divorced..." Everything was my fault according to his dad and grandparents. He was raised to believe that I had just abandoned him and his brother of my own free will. I tried to tell him that that wasn't true, but he was so brainwashed that I knew he didn't believe me. Daniel also implemented his dad's behavior – drinking, lying, stealing, and spending too much time behind bars. I didn't want him to end up like his father, but it seemed almost inevitable by the time he came to live with me.

Unlike Daniel, who takes after Don Jr., Steve takes after me. He is really good at connecting with people and animals, and he is fun and easy going. Despite all of the dysfunction in his upbringing, Steve turned out alright. He made his share of mistakes, but overall, he was honest with me and recognized when he was going down the wrong path. Steve grew up calling his stepmother "Mom," so he calls me Linda. It hurt my feelings that Steve wouldn't call me mom, but I understood. If we were around people who expected him to call me mom, he would, but it wasn't as often as I would have liked.

In a short amount of time, I realized that raising two teenage boys was very challenging. At one time, Daniel borrowed his boss's car, then drove it home drunk and sunk it into a riverbed. He also got stabbed once on his way home from a party. Steve didn't get into as much trouble, and he would oftentimes come to my defense if Daniel would go into a rage about me. In spite of all of the trouble, however, I wanted to create some happy memories with my boys too. We took a trip to Hearst Castle in San Simeon, California and spent a few days taking tours. On a different occasion, we went to Disneyland for the day and had a great time on all the rides.

When the boys first came to live with me, we were sharing my one-bedroom apartment, and it soon became apparent that we needed to get a bigger home. I got a loan for a house in Long Beach. It wasn't in the best area, but, at the time, it was what I could (barely) afford. Money was a concern for me now that I had to support two other people, but worry for my boys was affecting ability to focus at work, which was affecting my commissions. Often, I'd leave early or drop by the house in the middle of the day to check in and see what they were up to. I started doing this more often once I found out they had both stolen from me to get money for drugs. They took my 33's and my jewelry so they could buy crack – which broke my biggest rule. They should have been kicked out for this behavior, but I was lenient because the thought of losing them again so soon was too hard.

The boys had good and bad experiences in California, but unfortunately, there was more bad than good, mostly because of the decisions they were making with alcohol, drugs, and friends. Both of my boys knew that their life choices weren't leading them down a good path. Daniel decided to enlist in the Navy in May 1989, only a year and a half after coming to California. Steve made a similar decision, and he asked me to sign a form that would allow him to join the National Guard. He wanted to get away from all the bad influencers in the neighborhood and at school. He was 17 and didn't finish high school, but he earned his GED in the National Guard.

With both boys gone, and payments that I couldn't afford, I decided to sell my house for a small profit to avoid foreclosure. I needed a place to live, so I called Robert, and he rented me a one-bedroom apartment on Broadway Street. After ending my relationship with Ray, I had gotten used to living alone, but living with my boys for the past two years had made me forget how it felt, so it took me a while to adjust. I missed my boys terribly, but I was glad that they were trying to get their lives back on track. However, without that worry present, my focus came back and I was starting to make commissions again.

September 7, 1989 is a day I will never forget. I had had a long day of paperwork and showing homes. It was an exceptionally hot day, and I was exhausted. When I got home to my ground-floor apartment, I made myself some dinner, opened some windows, and watched TV for a while. I showered and got ready for bed at 11:00 pm, closing most windows, except for one in the dining area to keep cool during the night.

I was sound asleep, until I sensed something. At this point, it was 4 am. I was lying on my back, and when I turned my head slightly to my right, I saw a large man reaching for my purse, which was hanging on my coat rack.

I said, "You can take my purse, but there's no cash in it. I just went grocery shopping yesterday."

I had startled him, and he pulled his hand back – but he showed no signs of leaving. I reached for my robe at the end of my bed. My goal was to get out of my bedroom and escape, somehow, but getting out of my apartment wouldn't be easy. My bedroom was at the end of the hallway, opposite a utility room. The only ways out were the front and back doors, but the back door was blocked by the man. To get out, I would have to make my way down the hallway, through the dining area and living room, and out the door without being stopped—a nearly impossible task since the man was larger than me and standing in front of my door. There was nowhere to hide.

Having put on my robe, we walked together into the living room. My fear was so intense that I was shaking uncontrollably. When we got into the living room, we both sat down. I was in a chair, and he sat down on the couch across from me. This is when I realized that my dining room window was wide open, and the screen was off. "This is how he got in," I thought to myself.

Sitting across from him, I made some observations. He was 6'2", over 200 pounds, and of African American descent. He seemed laid back; there was nothing violent up to this point. I did my best to hold a conversation with him. His voice sounded commanding, authoritative, but calm. I'd never seen him before, but I soon found out he'd seen me.

"Do you have any kind of weapons on you?" I asked.

"No," he answered.

"Where did you come from?" I questioned.

"A party. I did some coke and drank. It was nearby," he responded.

"My drug of choice was marijuana," I responded, "but I'm clean and going to NA now."

I wanted to find some commonalities, distract him from thinking of doing anything worse. As we talked, I intensely looked him over, memorizing anything and everything about him. I noticed a mole on the side of his face and his short hair, but not much else. I thought to myself, "I will survive this—and get this guy arrested." Under my breath, I was praying, hoping that God would intervene.

During our conversation, he asked for an ashtray and some water. I handed him a glass ashtray and a glass – not plastic – cup of water in hopes of getting some fingerprints. Throughout this process, he followed me. We returned to the living room and talked some more while he drank the water and smoked a cigarette. At this point, he informed me that he'd been watching me for about three weeks. He saw me going to the beach in my bathing suit, and he had been stalking me.

My fears went from bad to worse, especially when I realized he knew I was alone that evening. I needed to get him out of my apartment, but how? I suddenly remembered I had $20 put away, so I offered it to him. He took it. "I'll pay back my mom. I owe her $6," he said. But who knows what he used it for.

"Is there anything else in the apartment that you want? Take anything," I said, trying to get him out.

"No."

He only wanted me.

Tears filled my eyes and ran down my cheeks. My body shook more fiercely than before. With his incessant following and my apartment layout, I knew there was no way to escape. I knew trying to fight him would only aggravate him, making matters worse.

"Don't scream," he said. "If you do, I'll tie you up and gag you."

Escorting me back to my bedroom, I prayed and hoped that he wouldn't become violent. My crying and shaking only escalated, but it didn't bother him. I knew he was about to rape me.

"Do you have any protection?" I asked as he was taking off his pants.

"No."

"I think I have a condom in my wallet. Can I check and see?"

"Yes."

"It's really for your protection. You don't know who I've been with," I said, convincing him that I was doing it for his own good.

He took the condom, opened my robe, and fondled me before saying, "Lie down on your back."

So, I did. He proceeded to orally copulate me first. After he finished that, he put on the condom, and we had intercourse. Because he had been snorting cocaine, I was worried that it might take a long time for him to climax. I wanted this nightmare to be over as quickly as possible. The cocaine didn't interfere, and about 10 minutes later, it was over. Even though it was only 10 minutes, it felt like an eternity.

"Can I go to the bathroom?" I asked after he had gotten off of me.

"Okay, but leave the door open."

I went in and left the door partially open. I was in disbelief. I saw myself in the mirror shaking like I was having a nightmare. I sat on the toilet and realized that the condom had stayed up inside of me. I carefully removed it and placed in between some towels. I wasn't sure if it would be useful to the police or not, but I thought I better let them decide that.

He had gotten what he came for.

He had another cigarette and asked, "What do you plan on doing when I leave?"

I replied, "The first thing I'm going to do is pray for you."

I told him he needed to leave so I could get ready for work, and to my relief, he got up and walked to the door. But before leaving, he turned to me.

"I should say I'm sorry, but I'm not." These words were piercing.

He walked out the front door and casually made his way down the sidewalk, as if nothing had happened.

I closed and locked the front door. Carefully, I closed the dining area window, being mindful of the potential fingerprints he could have left on it. I kept the window screen on the ground. I dialed 911 and looked at the clock. Six am. Two hours prior, this nightmare had begun. These were two of the longest hours of my life.

When the police arrived, I felt a sense of relief and safety. I was extremely tired and still shaking uncontrollably. I told them what had happened, forcing me to relive the last two hours. I gave them the condom.

"Is there anyone who could take you to the hospital to have a rape kit done?" they asked.

"Yes, my friend Robert."

I gave Robert a call. He came right away. On the way to the hospital, he tried to console and comfort me. After the examination was completed, he took me back to my apartment. There was no way I was staying there alone. I packed a bag of clothes and necessities and went to Robert's house – on the complete opposite side of town – for a few days.

I was a wreck, physically and emotionally. I couldn't work. The constant paranoia—wondering if he'd come back or if he was still watching me—prevented me from functioning normally. I knew I couldn't stay in that apartment. I needed to move. Luckily, Robert owned another apartment building across town, and there was a vacancy. I moved a week after the incident took place. Knowing the suspect wouldn't know where I was living gave me some peace, but until an arrest and trial took place, I felt uneasy.

Sixteen days later, I received a call from the police.

"We have some mugshots for you to look at. Are you able to come down to the station?"

My heart raced. I didn't know how I would handle seeing his face again. Sweating and shaking, I agreed to look at the pictures.

I went down to the station. Walking in, I was nervous but excited. Getting called meant they had found him. After studying him in the dim room that night, I knew I was looking for a mole on the side of his face, but I couldn't see it because of the shadows in the picture. I picked the wrong man.

At a later date, I again went to the station, and this time, I picked the right man. He was already in custody before I went to look at pictures the first time. His DNA and fingerprints were scattered around my apartment—on the window, the glass of water, the ashtray, and the condom—and the police had him on file from a previous arrest. Now I confirmed they had found the man who raped me, and I was informed that he lived nearby my Broadway apartment.

Now that I was officially a victim of a crime, a court advocate was appointed to me, and the prosecutor introduced me to the Victims of Crime program. Somehow, I had to get my life back in order after this incident, and the advocate suggested a rape support group. In my condition, I thought that it wouldn't hurt to talk to people about it in order to move on. I attended meetings for several weeks but stopped going because dwelling on bad experiences weekly was too draining.

Emotionally, the support group was helpful for a time, but the physical side effects of the incident persisted. Severe stress-induced neck and back pain limited my range of motion for several weeks. I hoped it would go away on its own, but a month afterwards, it persisted. I tried biofeedback on several occasions to try to relax, which provided temporary relief, but the pain came back. Ultimately, I visited my chiropractor three times a week for several weeks to help with the pain. The Victims of Crime program covered the cost of these visits.

As the case moved forward to trial, there was a preliminary hearing on October 5, 1989. I was put in contact with the D.A. and she said, "With the amount of evidence you obtained, this is the best rape case I've ever had," meaning it as a compliment to me. I was proud that I was able to obtain evidence during a traumatic experience that enabled me to put him behind bars. This pride was only elevated when I found out he had raped four other women. My actions helped bring peace and justice to those other victims. The D.A. contacted them, and each woman identified his mugshot. Since the other women hadn't collected evidence, the chances of him being caught were slim to none.

When the court date finally arrived, I was ready to testify. Anthony Simpson—my rapist—was going to be there, sitting in the courtroom, looking at me. I did not want to set my eyes on him ever again, but I wanted him put away. When I was called to the stand, I had to retell and relive that night. My voice was weak, and my body was shaking, but my desire to have him convicted was stronger than anything else. It was emotionally draining and difficult, but I did it. I had the four other women—four other victims—counting on me to put him away. They were in the courtroom with me to support me, which further motivated me to be strong.

Anthony Simpson was found guilty. He was turned over to the prison authorities January 30, 1990. The court set a sentencing date. I was looking forward to that day. It was the last time I would have to go into a courtroom and see him. When the day came, anxiety and anticipation filled every thought. The sentence was read—16 years in prison. Relief poured over the four other women and me. Knowing he would be off the streets and unable to hurt anyone else enabled us to begin to move on.

Two years after the rape, I got a call from the *Long Beach Press Telegram*. They asked if I would be willing to do an interview and tell my story about the rape. They said that by telling my story, I might be able to help other women and destigmatize the attitude about women coming forward after a rape or sexual assault. I gladly did the interview. The newspaper article was published on November 17, 1991. It covered the entire front page of that week's issue of the *Long Beach Press Telegram*, and continued on several inner pages as well.

Shortly after the newspaper article was published, I received a call from a TV producer named Ben who lived in Hollywood. He was working on a documentary called "Crimes Against Women" and he wondered if I'd come to his home so he could interview me. I drove there for the interview, and he had a room with lights and cameras all set up for me to tell my story. He said that once it was reviewed, he would use a couple segments of my story on the documentary. Unfortunately, it has never been aired on TV. We were ahead of our time. I recently reconnected with the producer, and we agreed that today's viewing audience would be more receptive to this subject matter. Even though the documentary has yet to be viewed by the public, I still feel that I did what I could to help myself and others with those interviews.

I have asked myself more than once, "Why did this happen to me?" I've concluded that the situation happened so I could prevent Anthony from raping other women. How I was able to collect evidence during this situation is hard to understand. I believe it had to have been divine intervention guiding me that night, helping me to intentionally collect fingerprints, DNA, and a physical description during such a traumatic event.

Decades later, I still wake up almost every morning around 4 am. I get up, check the window and door locks, and go back to bed. I've never slept with a window open again. In any public place, I am suspicious of men who look at me for too long, always keeping my pepper spray accessible. What angers me the most is that my home is no longer a place of comfort. Your home should be your sanctuary, a safe place to rest and relax. In any home I have lived in since then, I have not felt safe, regardless of where my home has been. On the doorknob of my bedroom, I keep a small windchime, and in my room, I keep an arsenal—a cattle prong, a can of wasp spray (with a 27 ft range), pepper spray, my grandfather's rifle, and my purebred Pitbull, Brooke. I was raped 31 years ago, but I was robbed of security for life.

Chapter 8: Smothered

My coworkers at Re/Max, where I was working at the time, were uneasy and didn't know what to say to me due to the rape. I tried to get back into the swing of work, but it was very difficult, so I ended up leaving. I made one last attempt to continue my real estate career. I thought maybe if I went to a different company and worked with new people, it might be what I needed, but it wasn't. I couldn't focus and work on commission anymore. I signed up with Kelly Services for temporary employment so that I had a paycheck at the end of the week. I also continued to go to NA meetings. Despite the trauma of the rape and court case, I did not go back to using marijuana. I remained clean and sober. Now more than ever I needed support and encouragement to stay on the right path.

After the rape, I wasn't interested in men. One night, I needed a meeting, and I had been encouraged by my sponsor to attend AA meetings to hear new stories and receive further support. That was where I met Ernie. I would talk to him after each meeting while we were all standing around socializing. Ernie was tall, about 6'2" and maybe 190 pounds. He had blue eyes, bushy eyebrows, a mustache, and curly light brown hair. He was originally from Oklahoma and worked with Texaco Oil Company.

After several conversations, Ernie asked for my phone number, and he called later that night and invited me out for dinner. We started dating shortly thereafter. He drove a truck, smoked cigarettes, went to horse races, and listened to country music – all of which were the complete opposite of my interests. Regardless of this, we had fun together. We liked going to nice restaurants and the NA and AA dances.

He was an old-fashioned kind of guy, a real gentleman. He'd have flowers delivered to my apartment constantly. Before one bouquet died, another would already be on its way. Pretty soon, my apartment looked like a funeral home. He would write me love letters, open my car door, and pull out my chair at a restaurant. Whenever I would stay over at his apartment, he would wake up early and make me breakfast in bed.

Ernie always wanted to buy me gifts for nothing in exchange, which was something that had never happened to me before. He once saw an outfit he thought I'd like, and he took me to the mall because he wanted me to try it on. He couldn't remember what store it was in when we got there, so he just told me to pick something out instead. I wasn't able to do it. I started getting hot and sweaty with anxiousness because I felt so uncomfortable in the moment, so we ended up just going home. He would still give me many surprise gifts, some of which included rose-shaped earrings, a pendant, and a ring. He also bought me a sweatshirt from Bakersfield, which was his hometown. My whole life, I have been self-sufficient, and if a man ever gave me anything, it was because he wanted something from me in return. Ernie wasn't like that.

After we'd been dating for a while, Ernie told me he'd like me to meet his dad, who lived in Bakersfield. His mom had already passed on. We went and stayed a couple of nights, and I met several other family members of his. I really liked all of them, and when we got back home to Long Beach, Ernie told me his dad said he's never seen him so happy. After telling me this, Ernie grabbed my hands and looked me in the eyes with a big smile on his face. He told me how much he loved me and asked me if I'd marry him, and I accepted. I knew we hadn't been dating for very long, but Ernie was a breath of fresh air. After my horrible relationship with Ray and the trauma of the rape, I felt safe with Ernie. Since the rape, I had remained celibate. No touching, not even to hold hands. It wasn't until I met Ernie that I had sex. I had told him about the rape, and he was very patient and sympathetic with me.

We got married in Bakersfield on September 22, 1990, which was just a little over a year after the rape. Most of Ernie's family lived in the area, and I had some family drive there from So Cal. My friend Norman and his wife took a train from San Francisco to be there, and my mom drove in from Nevada, where she was living at the time with my step-dad. To my surprise, my mom stayed in the dressing room with me to help me do my hair and fix my veil, but this show of affection made me happy. Even though this was my third marriage, it was Ernie's first. We had a nice ceremony in a local church. The reception hall was close by. The theme was a red rose in a vase on each table with black accents. We hired a catering service, and it was buffet style. We had a DJ there for our entertainment. My white '82 MBZ was decorated with a "Just Married" sign, and when we drove away, there was a string of cans attached to the car. We headed to the motel where we stayed for the night. We weren't able to go on any kind of a honeymoon right away, so the next day, we went to visit Ernie's dad for a while. One of Ernie's friends had heard about the rape and bought me a nice handgun. It was a quite unusual wedding gift but thoughtful under the circumstances. We went to the target shooting range so I could try it out. After that day, we had to drive back to Long Beach. We both had to get back to work.

A couple of months later, we were able to take time off of work for our honeymoon, so we took an all-inclusive trip to Ocho Rios, Jamaica. As soon as we landed and set foot on the ground in Jamaica, we had people approach us and offer us marijuana. We both declined because we were clean and sober. While we were there, we took a one-day trip to Dunn River Falls, visited all of the huts where people would sell things, and I even let a woman on the beach braid my hair. We had a wonderful honeymoon that lasted about a week, so we were a little sad to have to go back to reality.

While in Long Beach, I liked working out at the gym and running on the beach. Ernie would never come with me. I don't think Ernie had exercised since high school. His skin was fair and he didn't really like relaxing on the beach like I did. His daily routine consisted of getting up, reading the newspaper, eating breakfast, packing a lunch, and heading off to work. Occasionally, I'd get bored, so I would make banana bread and take some to him.

Even after we were married, Ernie used to write love letters to me quite often. They were nice, at first, but after a while, the number of flowers, "I love you's," and love letters became overkill. I found him to be almost too nice, and it was making me feel completely smothered. After about nine months of marriage, I made an appointment with my therapist who I'd been seeing for some time. She told me that if I wasn't happy and stayed with him out of guilt, I'd be untrue to myself and him. She also told me that I might have married him so quickly because he was so drastically different from anyone I'd ever dated. She suggested that we both come in and talk to her together. During our couple's therapy session, my therapist could tell Ernie really loved me, and he was crushed when he found out that I wasn't happy with him. I felt bad, but I was miserable and I didn't want to pretend that I wasn't, so I told Ernie that I wanted a divorce.

After facing the reality of another unsuccessful marriage, I decided I was ready to move on and get out of Long Beach. My friend Norman had his own business that he ran out of his house in the city of Lakeport. Once I let him know what was going on, he offered to let me stay with him and his wife and work for him. He ran a management consulting company.

Simply put, he was a headhunter. He would recruit people from one company and move them over to another company. The pay was commission but was quite handsome when you made a placement. It was all phone solicitation. I was good on the phone during my real estate career, and my friend thought I ought to be pretty good at this, too. I decided to give it a try. I let Ernie know that I was moving and I packed up and left. Even though I wasn't happy in our marriage, it was still difficult to say goodbye to him and drive off, but that's just what I did. About 10-12 hours later, I arrived in the small town of Lakeport, about 30 minutes east of Ukiah and about two hours south of the Oregon border. I was just minutes from Clear Lake. It was just beautiful up there, with its cleaner air and slower pace.

Once I got to Lakeport, it didn't take long to settle in. I was making phone calls from 8 am to 4:30 pm Monday-Friday. It certainly wasn't a fast-paced job like real estate, but it got me by. The longer I spent there, however, the more I started to miss my dysfunctional family in Michigan. I'd already experienced more than enough in California, and I was longing to go back home.

On December 14, 1991, a few weeks after I moved to Lakeport, I received a call from my only grandmother, Catherine. To get a long-distance call was a big deal, so I was surprised to hear from her. She asked how I was and so on, and we talked for about 10 minutes. The thing I remember most from our conversation that day was that before we hung up, she said "I love you." And I told her I loved her, too. That was the first, or at least the only time I can remember, that she said that to me. It was very special to me and something I will never forget.

Meanwhile, Steve had returned from the National Guard and moved back in with his friend in Long Beach. It was a rough neighborhood, and he wanted to get out of there. I didn't blame him—I didn't want to see him stay there either. I decided to move out of Norman's house and rent a downstairs apartment less than five minutes away, and Steve came to live with me. For a short time, I was managing the apartment building and living rent-free. In addition to my managing job, Steve and I found seasonal work at the Mount Konocti pear sheds.

In July 1992, I had plans – and an airline ticket – to go back to Michigan for a class reunion. Steve stayed in Lakeport. When I got there, I stayed with my aunt Beverly and uncle Tim – my two favorites. While I was there, they were very nice to me; they would make me breakfast and take me out to eat. This was one of the aunts who went to court against me in regard to custody of my boys. However, a lot of time had gone by and they knew about the rape in Long Beach. Maybe they just felt sorry for me.

I enjoyed my 20-year class reunion. It was the class of 1972 at Bangor John Glenn High School in Bay City, Michigan. It was interesting to see these people after such a long time and hear about their lives. While I was in Michigan, I made my rounds trying to see everybody that was important to me.

My maternal grandparents were two of the people I wanted to see on my visit. I was worried about my grandpa because he had been in the hospital right before I came to Michigan, and my grandma was also concerning me. She was becoming unpredictable in her old age. Prior to coming back to Michigan, I heard through the family grapevine that my grandma was interested in smoking pot to help with her arthritis. I didn't expect that my grandma would smoke weed, but she was a woman ahead of her time – wanting to use marijuana medicinally. I also didn't expect her to mix alcohol with pills, but she did. She was diabetic with high blood pressure and heart problems, so the doctor had her on valium, which she regularly enjoyed with a few cans of beer. With her, there were always surprises waiting.

During my visit, my cousin Shawn and I were heading to a NA dance. We both wanted to stop by and see our grandma and grandpa. I called and asked Grandpa if we could come by around 7 pm, and he agreed. We went over there, and as soon as Grandpa let us in the front door, Grandma started yelling at us for coming over during her favorite TV show. Grandpa stood there dumbfounded. As if that wasn't bad enough, she was so buzzed up from her valium and beer that she didn't even recognize my cousin. We explained that Grandpa said it was all right to come by, but she clearly wasn't interested in talking with us. We ended up leaving in tears. We had to pull ourselves together to go to the dance, where we had a good time.

The end of my vacation was drawing near, and I was on the west side of Bay City where my grandparents lived. The thought came to my mind to stop by and see them one more time, but I didn't. I hadn't called first, so I didn't want to stop by unannounced after the previous incident.

Luckily, I had visited with them when I first got to Michigan, before the class reunion. During this visit, I took a picture of my grandparents, which I was notorious for doing, and recorded a conversation with my grandma on my tape recorder. I usually would travel between Thanksgiving and Christmas, but the class reunion brought me back in July. I was very grateful to have been able to spend this time with my grandma because, one week after I got home, I received a phone call from my grandpa in Michigan. My grandma had died on July 30, 1992. Her death was totally unexpected, seeing how it was my grandpa who had been hospitalized when I'd first arrived, not her. I was shocked and upset, but I still had to work. I decided since I'd just gotten back from Michigan a week prior that I would not go to the funeral. I'd just seen her and I wanted to remember her that way.

I still have the recording I made with my grandma, but it's difficult to hear someone you love sounding so alive when in reality you know they're not physically here. Later, I realized my grandma was an alcoholic pill popper. Nevertheless, I loved her – bad habits and all.

Chapter 9: The Right Thing to Do

With Grandma gone, Grandpa was left alone. My family knew he was extremely lonely because my uncle would often see him sitting by himself in Vet's Park in Bay City, just looking at the water. I asked Steve if he would be willing to move back to Michigan to take care of Grandpa with me. Steve and I agreed that it was the right thing to do. We knew taking care of my grandpa would come with its challenges. My grandpa liked his beer and, sometimes, whiskey. He used to make a cup of instant coffee and dump some whiskey in it. He walked with a limp due to a broken hip, and he had emphysema. He was still able to take out the trash and walk his dog for a short distance, but that was about it. He still drove – I think he was 78 at the time – but he couldn't take care of himself. Grandma had done all the cooking and cleaning. The only foods Grandpa could prepare were microwave-baked potatoes, pickled herring and crackers for lunch, and maybe boil and egg or two. He had the money, but he was too cheap to go out and eat.

After the funeral, I called my grandpa and asked him what he planned on doing now that he was a widower. I wasn't sure if he'd move in with someone else or want to stay in the house. He said that he just wanted to stay where he was at, but he knew needed help. I asked him if he'd like Steve and I to move in with him. He said that sounded good to him, and we'd give it a try. I didn't necessarily want to leave Northern California. I loved the mountains, the ocean, and the warmer weather, and California had been home for 17 years. However, I didn't want to be so far away from my family anymore, and I was ready to go back.

In October 1992, Steve and I moved back to Michigan to stay with Grandpa. He'd been alone since the end of July, but we needed a few months to get our affairs in order. I rented a U-Haul truck equipped to tow the 1982 240D MBZ I still had. The Victims of Crime program, which supported me during the trial and conviction of my rapist, covered our moving expenses. Steve got his license at 19, but he was still apprehensive about driving because of the incident with sinking a car in the riverbed. All in all, he drove maybe 2 hours, leaving me to drive the rest of the long trip myself.

We arrived in Michigan on Election Day, November 2, 1992. It had been a long haul from Northern California. When we got there, I greeted Grandpa with a hug and a kiss on the cheek. He was 6'2" and had lost weight. At that time, he was about 190 pounds, but he weighed 225 when Grandma was still alive. Between my grandma's death and his lack of cooking skills, he looked frail and unhealthy.

My cousin had taken care of Grandpa a little bit, dropping off frozen meals and occasionally doing some light cleaning, but once she found out that we were coming, she stopped cleaning altogether, leaving quite the mess for us. The whole house had carpet. The kitchen and the utility room had indoor/outdoor carpet, while the bedrooms, bathrooms, and hallways had regular carpet. None of it looked like it had seen a vacuum in weeks. There were crumbs, dust, and dog hair everywhere. The counters were cluttered, and everything needed to be pulled out and cleaned thoroughly. Grandpa had taken care of the basics, which consisted of washing the dishes, doing the laundry, and cleaning the toilet bowl. But, all of my grandma's belongings remained untouched. Her toiletries, makeup, and other belongings were still in the second bathroom and in her closet. Aside from the messiness, it looked like she still lived there.

After settling into our new home, Steve and I needed to find work. I did some temporary work for Kelly Services. It was just before the holidays and they were usually looking for help that time of year. Steve used his experience from the National Guard and went into the communications field. He was putting up satellite dishes. He made good money but didn't really like working on icy, snowy roofs in the dead of winter.

When I wasn't working outside the home, I was cooking and cleaning. After a few weeks, I noticed that when I was cleaning or doing the dishes, my grandpa was watching me. I would turn around, and he'd be right there. Once, when both my hands were conveniently in the dish water, he put his hands on the top of my shoulders. I turned my head in his direction, and he leaned over and kissed me. I was in disbelief. I was angry. I was confused. He caught me completely off-guard, and I didn't know how to react.

A few days went by, and it happened again. He told me that I made life worth living. That's when I knew I had to put a stop to this. I'd come to take care of him because I thought it was the right thing to do, but I wasn't there to fill Grandma's shoes, especially in a sexual way. Even though we weren't blood relatives, he was my grandma's second husband and the only grandpa I'd known my whole life.

I had a hard time saying "No" directly to him, even though I knew this was wrong. This wasn't something that I expected, and I certainly didn't want any part of it. I was worried that he had a different agenda when I had offered to help take care of him. I wanted to handle the situation cautiously because the last thing I wanted was for Steve and I to get kicked out. My solution to this bizarre and uncomfortable situation was to avoid him. If I saw him coming my way, I'd dart off someplace else. Pretty soon, he took the hint and stopped pursuing me. Even several months after this, however, I was still walking on eggshells in case Grandpa got drunk and tried something again, but he never did. It took about a year before I started to feel comfortable in that house. What I'll never figure out is why he thought I'd go along with that kind of unacceptable behavior in the first place.

After about a year or so, Grandpa was happy and much healthier. He liked to eat three meals per day. He enjoyed my cooking so much that he gained weight, and he wouldn't ever go out to eat because that meant missing one of my meals. The closest thing I got to a night off in the kitchen was when he'd buy a rotisserie chicken from the local grocery store. Even then, I still had to cook side dishes and clean up. My aunt Kathy said I was a godsend. She knew how much I was doing to take care of her stepfather, and she appreciated my hard work, unlike her sisters who couldn't have cared less about how he was taken care of.

Because I took such good care of Grandpa, he wanted to make sure I stayed. Grandpa wasn't one to stay cooped up at home all day long, so it wasn't uncommon for him to run out to the grocery store once a day. One time, he was gone for quite a while. I wasn't sure where he went. I later found out that he went to see his attorney. As a retired GM employee of 32 years, he had access to free attorney services at the local 362 U.A.W. office, which was less than a mile away from his home.

When he finally got home, he stood just inside the front door holding paperwork in his hands, wobbling slightly due to his broken hip. He informed me that he had just changed his will and made me the beneficiary of his estate. I was stunned. I hadn't expected anything in return for my help. Not only was I surprised, I was concerned. I knew that once his four un-adopted stepdaughters found out, they were not going to be happy campers, especially my aunt Beverly. She was the youngest of the bunch and saw dollar signs wherever she looked. Her materialistic attitude was well-known in the family.

I knew Grandpa would be anxious to tell them about this drastic change to his will – he knew it'd get a rise out of them. He said the only time anybody ever bothered with him was on his birthday or holidays, so they didn't deserve to benefit from his estate.

There was one main stipulation that he made very clear in the will. I had to reside in his home at 807 Sidney Street in Bay City, Michigan until his death. So now I was the beneficiary, Steve was in second place, and my cousin Sharon was in third. When Grandpa told me what he did and I got copies of the will, I just knew without a doubt that one day, when Grandpa's time came, this will would absolutely be contested.

In the meantime, I needed to get some permanent work. Grandpa wasn't willing to give me money while he was alive. He'd tell me, "Once I'm dead, it's all yours." Even though I wasn't paying rent, I still needed clothes, cat food, car insurance, and other necessities. Money wasn't the only reason I wanted a job. I needed to get out of the house more. It was difficult to be stuck there all day every day with Grandpa, especially since he had made sexual advances toward me. I found work doing in-store demonstrations at a local grocery store.

After doing store demonstrations for a couple weeks, my supervisor asked me if I'd be interested in doing store resets, which paid more. A reset is when you take everything off the grocery store shelves, clean them, and move the shelves, if necessary. Then, using a list that tells you how to organize product, you would reposition the items on the shelves. The last step was to replace the product labels. I'd never done that before, but I was excited to have an opportunity to learn something new. Once I realized how much I liked it, I found full-time employment working for Accessories Associated, Inc. (AAi) in 1994. I traveled all over Michigan to different stores, acting as merchandiser and supervisor for the part-time help.

There were times when I'd be gone overnight, sometimes for two nights and three full days. I'd purchased day passes to local gyms when I was visiting different cities; even though I was busy, I still always found time to work out and continue self-care. There was independence with this job, which is something I craved considering my living situation with Grandpa.

AAi would have an annual national meeting for all their employees. At this meeting, employees had the opportunity to submit ideas for Profit Improvement with a chance to win money for good suggestions. I suggested that the sale tags for the products be designed like bread-bag clips so that they could be easily slipped on without having to remove all of the product from the hooks. My suggestion won, and I received $500, which made me very proud. The company told me that even though I'd only been there a few months, it was a veteran-like idea and it was featured in the monthly newsletter. My idea was implemented right away.

After a while, driving all over Michigan and taking care of Grandpa at home made me burn out quickly. I didn't have as much time for myself as I would have liked. I wasn't the only one who wasn't happy with the caregiving job, though. In my absence, Steve learned just how much work it was to take care of Grandpa. After coming home one day, I noticed a card in my bedroom. The cover had a picture of a scruffy dog on it, and it read, "Things got a little hairy around here while you were gone." Inside, the card said, "Glad you're home." Steve wrote a note below the card's message, which read, "I didn't realize how much you do for Grandpa." I could tell he really appreciated how hard I worked for those that I care about, and it was refreshing to have him acknowledge that.

Steve told me a few of the funny stories about his time taking care of Grandpa while I was gone. On one of the days, Steve, who liked staying up late, was sleeping until about 11 am. He slowly got up and opened his bedroom door. He could see that Grandpa was in the kitchen, holding a crumb-filled bread bag in his hand. Steve watched as Grandpa looked to the left and to the right, but he didn't see Steve watching him. Grandpa turned the bread bag upside down and shook it all over the counter. That's what Steve gets for not being up to make Grandpa's lunch. Steve didn't tell Grandpa he saw this little act of revenge, but he told me.

After working for AAi for 10 months, I realized that I was working way more than 40 hours per week, so my salary pay wasn't enough. I'd constantly be busy with inventory, sales, new planograms, or markdowns, so there was always something to be done. I gave my supervisor a three-week notice, and I was able to leave on good terms.

I still needed money, so I found a job as a fitness instructor at an all-women's gym. I worked out at this gym frequently, so I was excited for the opportunity to work there. Fitness has always been a constant part of my lifestyle– I have been weight lifting and running since 1981, and I am familiar with all kinds of gym equipment. The pay was little, maybe $6 an hour at that time, but I loved the job. It didn't even feel like work to me, and it was only 5 minutes from my house. After having such good sales training in my real estate career, selling gym memberships was easy. In addition to liking the job, I got a free membership and free tanning. I worked there for about a year and a half. I asked for a raise, but they told me that they were already paying me all that they could. I was pretty much already running the place and there wasn't any opportunity for promotion. I gave notice and left on excellent terms.

Once again, I was on the hunt for a job. I prefer to work independently, and something that I did learn from my mother was how to be a good housekeeper. My youngest sister Pam worked as a housekeeper, but she had COPD and would run out of breath frequently, so I started my housekeeping work by helping her out. Eventually, I started working on my own, and when housekeeping become to much for Pam, I took over her work as well. Cleaning wasn't my favorite fallback job, but at least I was good at it and had the independence I wanted.

Grandpa was very tight with his money. When Steve and I first moved in with Grandpa in 1992, I think he had maybe $8,000 and still had a small mortgage on the house. He did eventually pay off the mortgage and was able to save – unlike me. Between all the different jobs I had tried out and the cleaning jobs I was working, I wasn't bringing in enough money to pay for my needs, so I decided to ask Grandpa for some compensation. I did my best to make my case for why I deserved the money. I made a list of all of the chores I did for him – cooking, cleaning, laundry – and let him know how much it would cost if he had to pay someone else to come in to do this work for him, which totaled $350 a week. I requested only $100 a week, which was really quite generous on my part. I left the note on his recliner. When he saw it and read it, he refused to pay me for my work. Again, he told me that when he was dead, everything that he owned would be mine.

The note backfired. Not only did I not get any money, but Grandpa took it over to greedy Aunt Beverly's house. She kept the note. I was upset with Grandpa for giving it to her, but I'm sure he didn't know the damage it could cause.

Living with and caring for an elderly person can be difficult, and very demanding of your time, if you are putting that person before yourself. I loved my grandfather very much. He was the only grandparent that I had left. And I would have done anything for him, but sometimes we all need a break.

On a beautiful spring day, Steve and I went to the local mall to the movie theater. After we got there, we weren't able to see the show because the tickets were sold out. So, we turned around and went right back home. We were gone 10 or 15 minutes – the mall was very close by. When we arrived, Grandpa was holding a wash rag over the bridge of his nose. He also had some other scratches and blood on his face. We were shocked at how he could have gotten so roughed up in such a short amount of time.

While we were gone, the paperboy had come by to collect. When Grandpa heard the knock and saw the paperboy, he got up in a hurry. Grandpa's dog was barking like crazy as Grandpa scurried to the door. In his hurry, Grandpa tripped on the only throw rug in the house, and he fell face first into the storm door. Neither one of my grandparents liked throw rugs because they worried about tripping over them, and they were clearly right to keep them out of the house. Luckily, his injury looked worse than it was, and I cleaned and bandaged him up. Accidents like this became more frequent. Another time, Grandpa fell in his bedroom. He tripped and bumped into his dresser. His skin was thin, and he bruised very easily. I was starting to get worried about him. Steve and I tried to make sure that one of us was home at any given time, just in case something happened.

It took a lot to persuade my grandpa to spend money and go out to eat, but, if it wasn't on his dime, he was all for it. So, one night, Steve and I took Grandpa out to Linwood Corners, a buffet restaurant we all enjoyed. It was a good variety of home cooking at a good price, and with Grandpa's appetite, an all-you-can-eat-buffet was always a favorite.

After we were seated, we told the waitress we were all going to have the buffet. The restaurant was set up so that the buffet area and dining area were separated by one step, which wasn't a problem for most people. Grandpa, on the other hand, didn't do so well with this step. When he was returning to the table with two heaping plates of meat and potatoes, he missed the step and fell face first onto the floor. Food was scattered around him, but he wasn't hurt in any way. Well, maybe his pride. Steve and I had to help him up, one of us on each side. Once he was up and dusted off, he went right back to the buffet to refill two plates, but this time, he cleared the step and enjoyed his meal. I was looking forward to a relaxing night off to eat, but of course, something had to go wrong.

Besides some trouble with Grandpa's clumsiness, life had been going fairly well since I'd moved back to Michigan. For the first time in a long time, I was uninvolved with men and much happier without them. After all the abuse and harassment that I'd endured, I was glad to be left alone. Unfortunately, I can't control other people, so this harassment-free time didn't last forever. In the late 90s, I decided it was time to sell my white MBZ 240D sedan. I loved that car, but Michigan winters didn't love it as much. The salt started taking its toll on the tire wells of the car, and it had a hidden leak. When it rained, water came in from somewhere – always in the same place on the floor of the passenger's side back seat – but no one could find out exactly where it was coming from. I'd have to keep the carpet pulled up so it wouldn't get soaked. I didn't know how easy it would be to sell it because Michigan is a GM state and the car was 16 years old. I placed an ad in my local newspaper and received one call from a guy and his wife who lived in the thumb area of Michigan. I set up a time for them to come by, and when they showed up to look at it, Steve and I went outside to talk to them. They loved the car, bought it, and went on their merry way.

Months went by, and one day there was a knock at the door. I believe my son was working and my grandpa was at the store, leaving me home alone. The buyer of the car was standing outside the door. I thought this was very strange, since we hadn't been in contact since the sale. When I opened the door, he mentioned that he was in the area, so he thought he'd stop by. A red flag went up in my mind. He really had no reason to stop by. If there was a problem with the car, he could have just called me. I was especially concerned after he told me this wasn't the first time he'd stopped by.

I had stepped outside when I had opened the door because I didn't want him coming in the house. After explaining his previous "visit," he leaned forward and tried to kiss me. I backed away in confusion and disgust. I said, "What the hell are you doing? Leave and do not come back." Without a reply, he turned around and left. I stood there baffled. I had no clue why he thought that would be permissible. I went inside, shut the door, and locked it. With my past experiences, I feared the worst – what if he was stalking me? But, I never saw him again.

Not long after the creepy car guy tried to kiss me, I received another unexpected visitor at the door. This time, Grandpa was home. When I answered the door, I found a very professional-looking woman who I had never met before. She explained that she was a social worker from Adult Protective Services and wanted to speak with Grandpa. Confused yet cordial, I let her in and walked her over to where Grandpa sat in his lazy boy recliner with his dog on his lap. She asked if they could speak privately, so he got up from his chair, and they went to his bedroom where they sat on the edge of the bed to talk. Because this was such a weird situation, I was very curious as to what they were talking about. I know I shouldn't have, but I stood and eavesdropped by the door.

She was asking questions about how my son and I were treating him. Grandpa was just as confused as I was, until she mentioned the reason she was there. Someone had called Adult Protective Services and made allegations that I was physically abusive, that he was restricted from using a portion of the house, that I had coerced him into putting my name on the bank account as beneficiary, and that I had forced him to put my name on the title of the house. All of this was untrue.

The evidence this "anonymous" caller gave for abuse had to do with some bruises on Grandpa's arm. He was a clumsy, easily bruised, elderly man. Even when doing the simplest task, he could end up with a bruise. Half the time, I would ask him how he got bruised, and he told me, "Oh hell, I don't know." For the particular bruises in question, he told the caseworker they were from when he was getting the mail. The mailbox was long and narrow, so his forearm would always hit the cover when he reached in.

As far as his living space, he could go wherever he wanted. However, we did put a child safety gate up by the hallway at the opposite end of the house, where Steve and I had our bedrooms and bathroom. We needed the gate because Grandpa didn't let his dog out frequently enough, and we didn't want dog pee all over the house. Grandpa didn't mind the gate, and it didn't prevent him from reaching the thermostat that was on the wall in the small hallway, which was the only thing he needed to access past the gate. Plus, he told her that he had a car in the driveway and could come and go as he pleased. At the time of her visit, he had just renewed his license.

The financial allegations were easy to refute. Grandpa told the caseworker that he chose to leave everything to me out of his own free will. He made it clear that I had never asked for that, and he went even further by sharing how grateful he was that Steve and I had moved in. He said that if it weren't for me and Steve moving in from California, he'd probably be in a nursing home. In her report, the caseworker noted that the step-daughters weren't happy about his "financial arrangements," and that his step-daughters only visited "maybe once or twice a year at holidays." My grandfather was very upset about this visit, and so was I. We both knew who was behind it: Aunt

Beverly, the greedy one trying to cause trouble for me. With Grandma gone for five years now, she figured his time would be up soon, and she was seeing dollar signs.

After 7 years of helping me take care of Grandpa, Steve had saved up enough money to buy his first home. He would still occasionally come over to help out if I was going to be gone for a while, but I missed having him around. Even though Grandpa hadn't done anything for a long time, his initial sexual advances were still in the back of my mind. I wasn't very excited to be home all alone with him.

After my experiences driving from place to place for work during the Michigan winters, I decided I should work a job where I just went to one place and home. I'm a jack-of-all-trades and a master of none, with an extensive list of 60-some job experiences.

One day I was on the phone applying for a teller position at the local bank. When we got to the question of whether or not I had a high school diploma or GED, I said no. She said the interview stopped there, but that if I took my GED to get back to her. That was the first time that not having my GED caused me not to get the job. I'd been putting it off for years, but I decided it was about time I got it. And I went to take a couple of practice tests, and the woman at the test center checked them and told me that I didn't need to take any more.

"You're ready," she told me.

I said, "I am?" but I took her word for it.

She set up a test date for me. I was most nervous about some of the math, but I went for it anyway. After I was done, I felt pretty good about the test. I had to wait for the test results by mail.

I went to visit a friend over the weekend. She lived out of town and I spent the night. The next day, I received a call from Steve that there was a letter there in regard to my GED. I told him to open it. To my surprise, he read me the scores and I passed very nicely. I actually scored quite high. The women commented to me that she hadn't seen such high scores in a long time, which made me feel great.

After I returned home from my visit, I realized that Grandpa's appetite started to change. I was used to preparing three meals a day for him, but he stopped eating and told me that he wasn't hungry. This was the man that shook breadcrumbs all over the counter because his lunch was late, so I knew something was wrong. I encouraged him to make an appointment with his doctor, and he agreed. A few days later, he went to his appointment, and the doctor felt he needed to be hospitalized. More tests were done on him, and the doctors discovered that on top of his existing emphysema, he now had pancreatitis. All I knew about pancreatitis was that it had something to do with your stomach. I didn't realize just how bad this was, especially for an 87-year-old man. I was very concerned and upset that this illness had suddenly snuck up on him. He was fine one day, and then the next day it seemed like everything had changed.

He stayed in the hospital from Monday until Friday. Every day that he was in the hospital, I went to see him. My days consisted of getting up, getting ready, visiting Grandpa, and going home to eat and let the dog out. The days went by quickly, but they were hard. It's not easy to watch someone who you take care of quickly decline in health. It all felt like a bad dream.

One day, I took my mom up with me to see him. We took turns to visit with him so that he wouldn't feel overwhelmed. While I was visiting with him, he took off his oxygen mask. I told him to put it back on. He said to me, "What's the point?" I helped him to put it back on anyway because we both wanted him to be able to get back home. Going home was his incentive for keeping it on. That's when I leaned over and hugged him and said, "I love you, Grandpa," and he said, "I love you, too, Ging." In my family, we stuffed our feelings, but this time I wasn't going to hold back. At that point, I knew he didn't have much time left so I wanted to make sure he knew that I loved him.

The doctor told me that they would keep Grandpa comfortable. In other words, he was dying. He knew it. We all knew it. He wanted to be at home, and I don't blame him. To allow him to come home, we needed to have a hospital bed for him. I called hospice and they came over with the bed on Friday, the day he was scheduled to be discharged.

On top of Grandpa's decline, my uncle had a heart attack at Lowe's and died on the Sunday before Grandpa went into the hospital. As if things weren't already hard enough, I had to deal with the loss of one of my favorite uncles. I went to his funeral, but Steve and I didn't go to the cemetery because we wanted to get back to Grandpa.

Friday afternoon at about 4 pm, we got Grandpa home. He laid in the hospital bed that was set up in his living room. With his dog at his side and the TV remote in his hand, he was happy, as happy as he could be anyway. Grandpa wasn't supposed to get out of bed. He was wearing adult diapers now and had a urinal to use right in his bed. I knew it was going to be a long night. My mom spent the night with Steve and me. Even though we didn't have the best relationship, I was glad to have her there with us.

Everybody went to bed and tried to sleep. I felt like I was just lying there with one eye open and my ears tuned to any sounds of Grandpa getting up. He was a big man and not too easy to pick up. Sure enough, I heard the rail on the side of the bed go down and he wanted to get up and go to the bathroom. Much to his dismay, I didn't let him get up. Instead, I helped him unfasten his diaper and use the bedside urinal. This is when we realized he had already wet the bed prior to this bathroom "trip," so my mom and I had to change the sheets while he was still in bed. My mom had experience with this from her work as a nurse's aide.

I didn't get much sleep at all. I was up very early. I sat next to the bed thinking about how I was losing my grandpa. Two weeks prior he was out driving himself around town, and now he was dying. It was hard to wrap my head around. I thought about how I had taken care of him for almost 10 years, and now that was coming to an end. I felt so helpless. I could see that his breathing was getting more labored. I went to the bedroom to wake up my mom. She said that she didn't think he had much more time. I called my sister Deborah and my brother-in-law Jim. Unlike my other relatives, Deborah would come over and visit with Grandpa outside of the holidays, so I thought she should be there to say goodbye. They lived about 10 minutes away, so they showed up quickly and both went over to talk with him.

They say that a person's hearing is the last thing to go, even if they're not responding. We all told him we loved him and were there for him. He died at 10 am the morning of Saturday, August 25, 2001, just a week after visiting the doctor.

Without thinking, I called the Medical Emergency number. But he was dead – all I needed to do was call the coroner. The coroner arrived and removed his body from the hospital bed after covering him with a sheet. I cried as they took him away, knowing that he wouldn't return to his home again. Once he was gone, I called to have the hospital bed picked up. It was only there for one day, but it was worth it. I was there to take care of him, so helping him to be comfortable in his home up until his last breath was important.

I was an emotional wreck. I lost the only grandfather I had ever known at the age of 47 – he was 87. Now I had to take care of the funeral. We had discussed the funeral arrangements in advance. He already had a plot paid for next to my grandma, and the headstone just needed his death date added. Grandpa was ethnically Jewish, so I asked him about embalmment, since Jewish people aren't usually embalmed. In his typical fashion, he replied, "Hell, I'll be dead. It don't matter." I knew he had been concerned about grave robbers, so I had asked whether he had wanted to be buried with his wedding ring, and he had said no; he wanted me to have it.

Even with the arrangements Grandpa and I had already discussed, there was still more to be done. Steve went with me to the funeral home to pick out a casket and all the rest of the necessary things. I knew some people had to come from out of town, so the showing lasted for three days. It was a long three days. We drove to the cemetery, where there was a 21-gun salute for Grandpa. The booming of the gunfire made me even more emotional. To see the service members saluting him and showing him the honor and respect he deserved really moved me, and my crying only got worse.

After leaving the cemetery, my brother and sisters planned to meet Mom and me back at Grandpa's house. However, Aunt Beverly invited all of us out to share a meal at Krysiaks, a local Polish restaurant. My siblings said no immediately; they didn't want to put up with her. My mom and I were hesitant, so she begged us to join her. We eventually gave in and met her at the restaurant. I wasn't very hungry because I was grieving. I picked at my food and ate a bit, but I was so emotionally drained that I didn't engage much in conversation. Physically, I was there, but emotionally, I wasn't present. If I had been more alert, I wouldn't have gone with Aunt Beverly. Looking back, this was her way of playing nice before what I knew would be coming – the contesting of Grandpa's will. She even paid for our meal, which was a big sign that she had a different agenda in mind. By the time we got back to Grandpa's house, my siblings were gone. I couldn't blame them for leaving; I wouldn't have wanted to wait either.

My mom and I unloaded some of the flowers from the funeral into the house, then I took my mom back to her apartment. When I got back home, it was empty. No Grandpa, just a lot of beautiful flowers. The recliner that Grandpa was sitting in just days ago was now empty. There was no one to cook for, besides myself. I couldn't believe he was really gone. No matter if you know that it's coming or not, death is never easy to deal with. Now my reason for returning to Michigan had been fulfilled. Now what to do? I felt a huge void in my daily life. While I decided what was next, I had to take care of the rest of Grandpa's affairs.

Right after Grandpa died, I decided to get the locks changed because I didn't know who might have had a key to the house and I didn't want people coming to take things without my knowledge. When I got home one day, I saw my mom trying to get into the house, but she soon discovered her key didn't work. What she was after, I have no idea. I'm sure she wasn't too happy that I was a step ahead of her.

A week after Grandpa's funeral, I went to the mailbox and there was a letter from an attorney, and it wasn't Grandpa's. I opened the letter and saw that my wonderful aunts, uncles, and my own mother were contesting the will. They all had their hands out now that money was in the mix, but their hands certainly weren't out when they had the opportunity to take care of him. I was the one who left my life in California, and this was the reward I got – a court case while I grieved his death. I wasn't surprised by the actions of my aunts and uncles, but I was surprised by my mom. She let her sister persuade her to take their side because she was so certain that they were going to win.

My mom's betrayal hurt me the most. I didn't see how my mom could agree with Aunt Beverly. My mom lived close by and came over one day per week to help me clean Grandpa's bedroom, so she knew I wasn't there to manipulate him and take his money. I was hoping that when the time came, she'd just stay neutral and when probate court was over, then I'd give her some money. But no, Aunt Beverly was very convincing, and she also had another motive. Aunt Beverly wanted my mom to help pay for the attorney fees, win or lose. My mom was on a fixed income. She didn't have a lot of money, but that didn't matter to Aunt Beverly. If there was a way she could get money, she would do it.

In the meantime, a hearing took place. The letter that I had written Grandpa years before his death was a key reason that the judge decided to move forward with the trial. This was the letter that I outlined how much my services would cost if he paid someone else to come in to do them – the one that he had given to Aunt Beverly. She was using it against me now, and, to my surprise, it was working. And even though I was listed as the beneficiary on Grandpa's bank account, the judge put a stay on the account until the jury trial was over. Until then, I got just $3K to live on. I didn't know how long the court process would be, so I needed to get a job to ensure that I would be financially stable.

Just walking distance from Grandpa's house was a new strip center with a Subway restaurant. I like working with people and food, so I went and applied. I got hired as a "sandwich artist," which was the most ridiculous job title I've ever had. As a licensed realtor, I was certainly over-qualified for the job, but I needed a job to stay afloat during this bizarre time. I had many different tasks to do, from baking the bread and the cookies to prep work and washing dishes – whatever needed to be done. I didn't care. I just wanted to stay busy, and it was hard to concentrate at times because of the stress that my so-called family was putting on me – again. This was the second time they'd taken me to court, and it hurt just as much as it did the first time.

On top of my own upcoming court case and grieving the loss of my grandfather, I was dealing with the legal troubles of both of my sons. After leaving the Navy, Daniel had continued to earn quite a rap sheet for himself, and he was in jail awaiting sentencing, probably being sent back to prison. Often times, I wouldn't tell people that I had two sons because I was embarrassed to say that he was in jail or prison again. Even though he let me down, I still kept in constant contact with him. While Daniel's legal troubles were upsetting but not very surprising, Steve had gotten into trouble around this time, too. This was Steve's first offense; as I prepared to go to court over the will, Steve was also preparing to go to court. There was too much going on all at once, but I couldn't do anything about it.

I now lived alone in Grandpa's house with his dog and my cat. I wanted all of this to be over, but it was unfortunately just beginning. Instead of being friendly and outgoing, I was stressed and uptight. My friends at the gym where I worked out noticed this difference, too, but no one could really do anything about it – only time could make it better. I continued working out, working various jobs for Kelly's Services, walking the dog, and taking care of Grandpa's belongings. It was a terrible time, full of uncertainty, and grief. I had to keep pushing forward one day at a time, like I had always done. I was in close contact with my attorney, trying to prepare for the trial. I was upset that I even needed an attorney, considering that I had done nothing wrong, but my family left me no choice.

At the end of October 2001, Steve and I took a much-needed vacation to Cancun, Mexico. This was the first vacation I'd taken since 1990, so it was long overdue. We got a pet-sitter to watch my dog and cat while we were gone. We had a wonderful and relaxing time, and I enjoyed the sunshine and the break from cooking and cleaning. I did my best to have fun, but I wasn't able to forget about the mess that was awaiting me back home. I was still grieving the loss of my grandpa, and I was awfully mad at my mom and her sisters. The contesting of the will was ridiculous, and I kept thinking of the upcoming legal issues that were only happening because of greed. Before I knew it, it was time to return back to Michigan.

When I returned home, there was a note from the pet-sitter along with my bill. The note went something like this: *Your mother stopped by one day while I was here, and she told me, "You better hope you get your money because there's a court case coming up and I don't think she'll be able to pay you." I'm a little concerned, so I'll return your house key after I get paid.* I contacted her and paid her immediately, so the issue was resolved, but it was clear that my mother was trying to cause me even more grief.

As if the stress of my grandpa's death and my court hearing wasn't enough, I was told that my step-mom Sandy, who was at an AFC, was having problems swallowing, so they had set up a doctor's appointment to get this looked at. Three days before her appointment, she choked on her lunch. She was rushed to the hospital where she died on March 28, 2002 at 58 years old. She was cremated after the showing and buried on my dad's grave.

The court date was approaching quickly. My family and I all had to meet together for my attorney to talk to my aunts and mother to take depositions. It only added insult to injury that I had to pay $600 for their statements in addition to my own legal representation, even though they were the ones taking me to court.

The only person in my family who stood up for me was my aunt Kathy. When my aunt Kathy was questioned, every answer was, "I can't dignify that." At the time, I was confused why she kept saying that, but I got a sense that she didn't want any part of this. Years later my suspicions were confirmed from my cousin Sharon; Aunt Kathy didn't want to testify against me, which is why she gave those answers.

My attorney suggested that I give my family something to maybe keep this from going any further. I was reluctant about doing so because I felt that that would make me look guilty of the accusations my aunt made about me. Well, I decided I'd throw them a bone of $1K each. As I expected, they rejected the offer. Now I was looking at a two-day jury trial.

In the meantime, I found out from Deborah that my aunt Annie was having her daughter drive by the house from time to time, to see if I spent any of the money and bought myself a new car. You'd think, by the way they were acting, that they were homeless or going hungry. Two of my uncles worked for the GM factory and the other two worked for the city. They lived comfortably. All this was about was pure greed. Unlike my aunts, my mother was drawing her husband's social security and had the least amount of income. She was the only one hurting for money, which is why I told her from the beginning to stay out of it. If she had listened to me, I would have gladly helped her out afterwards, but she chose her side and betrayed me, yet again.

On the first day of the trial, it was a very cold, snowy winter day. I wasn't sure if the hearing would take place because the road conditions were so horrible, but it did. Immediately, I could feel the tension in the court room once I saw my so-called family sitting on the opposing side. At the beginning of the trial, my aunts testified against me. Their lawyer brought up every allegation that was made against me, questioning them about each aspect. They were trying to paint a picture for the jury, making me look abusive and greedy. My aunts tried to use anything and everything against me. At one time, in a casual conversation before Grandpa had died, I had mentioned to my aunt Annie that Grandpa had legally changed his last name from his dad's last name to his mother's maiden name. Aunt Annie tried to use that in court as a reason why the will wouldn't be valid because he wasn't who he claimed to be. Well, I had found the original document of the name change prior to telling my aunt and had immediately sent a copy to my attorney. She tried to outsmart me, but I had the paperwork to prove her wrong. They tried to work every angle they could, but it wasn't going to work.

When it was my attorney's turn to speak, he called into question Grandpa's obvious independence. My aunts confirmed that Grandpa had his own car and could go wherever he wanted to, which didn't support their claims that I controlled Grandpa. Every allegation against me was put to rest once my attorney finished his line of questioning. At the end of the first day, I felt hurt. It was difficult to see my family take the stand against me. Sitting there hearing them spread lies and make me out to be the villain was upsetting, to say the least. Even though it hurt, I wasn't afraid. I knew I'd win the case, but I just wish I didn't have to hear all of their exaggerations and insults in the process.

On day two, it was my turn to take the witness stand. One of my few supporters, Steve, wasn't allowed in the courtroom when I testified because my attorney wasn't sure if Steve would also need to testify. As I approached the witness stand, I was a little nervous; I had seen enough crime TV to know how a prosecutor could twist someone's words. More than nervous, I was angry that I even had to be on trial in the first place. After I was sworn in, my attorney handed me a picture of my grandpa. I wasn't expecting this. I was prepared to be questioned, since I knew this day was coming, but I didn't know my attorney would start his questions with this.

He said, "Tell me who that is."

I said, "That's my grandpa."

I hadn't seen many photos of him since his death, so holding that picture in the courtroom brought me to tears. He had made his point. My tears were evidence enough that I cared for him. My attorney still asked me some questions, of course, but my reaction to Grandpa's picture showed the jury right away that I wasn't in it for the money.

After I was questioned, it was time to question Grandpa's UAW attorney. In about 18 months, he'd been over there 32 times. They knew who my grandpa was quite well. When the UAW attorney was questioned, he explained that Grandpa was very competent and knew what he was doing. He also told the jury that Grandpa had always visited him alone. The only time I went with Grandpa to the attorney's office was when he asked me to come to sign paperwork to appoint me as the executor of the estate, which was a decision Grandpa had made. The UAW attorney told the court that if anybody was coerced, it was me because of the stipulation Grandpa made about me staying in his house until his death.

Next, the case worker from Adult Protective Services was called to the stand. She testified that the complaint that was made was unwarranted and the case was closed. By the time the jury heard all of the testimony, they came to a decision and, $15K in legal fees later, I won the case unanimously. I stuck to my guns and now what Grandpa wanted would be fulfilled. When the judge gave the verdict, Steve heard one of my uncles say to the other, "I think we just lost." Yes, they had lost.

They had an opportunity to appeal the case, and they had a certain amount of time to file the paperwork. Their deadline was 4:00 p.m. on a certain day. I was pacing the floor and watching the clock on that day, feeling nervous and a little bit hopeful. As it got closer to 4:00 p.m., I still hadn't gotten a call from my attorney. It was hard to believe, but I thought that maybe they'd let it go and would leave me alone. A few minutes before 4, my phone rang. When I picked it up, I heard my attorney's voice. Hearing his tone of voice as he greeted me on the phone, I knew what had happened. "They filed the paperwork, didn't they?" I asked, knowing what the answer would be. He told me that they filed. I felt betrayed and hurt, knowing that my family had intentionally gotten my hopes up. They were hoping to win with a different attorney, but the new attorney they hired knew they wouldn't win after reading the court transcripts. The case was finally dismissed on December 17, 2002. I got access to my Grandpa's bank account as of January 15, 2003.

There were times when I wondered how things would have gone for me if I would have just stayed in California and lived my life. And there were many times I wished Grandpa wouldn't have made me the beneficiary. I had had a better relationship with my family when I came home for visits from California, but now I was back to square one.

My relationship with my Aunt Beverly and Uncle Tim deteriorated after the court case, and we didn't speak for years. In 2007, Aunt Beverly was diagnosed with cancer on the right side of her face, and she was told she would have about 5 more years to live. I spoke with her a short while after this, and we had a decent conversation, but Uncle Tim was still very standoffish because of his grudge against me. In January of 2013, Aunt Beverly became very sick, and she was admitted to the hospital. I wanted to go and see her, but I was told by my sister Deborah that Uncle Tim didn't want me to come to the hospital, so I told Deborah to please tell Aunt Beverly that I loved her. Deborah gave her my message and told Aunt Beverly that I wanted to come and see her, but Uncle Tim wouldn't allow it. My aunt mumbled something back to Deborah, but

Deborah didn't understand what she was trying to say, and I'll never know.

Aunt Beverly died on February 5, 2013. Deborah called and told me, and when I asked her when the funeral would be, she said that Uncle Tim didn't want me to come. I wasn't surprised, but I was still hurt. I considered Uncle Tim's wishes, but I decided to go anyway. I don't think it's right for a person to deny someone the opportunity to pay their last respects to a loved one. I got myself dressed and headed to the funeral home. I was fashionably late and everyone was already seated, so I sat alone in a small room with an intercom system in it so I could still hear everything. When the service was over, I walked into the main room where everyone was gathered. Uncle Tim just looked at me and didn't say anything at all. I was glad he didn't make a scene. My aunt was cremated, so I didn't even get to see her face one more time. Uncle Tim invited everybody – except me – to a local restaurant following the service, so I went home alone.

In September 2019, I heard that Uncle Tim was in the hospital. My mom and I had gone up to see him, and he smiled and was very cordial with me. Despite everything that happened, I told him he was still my favorite uncle. I was glad we were back on good terms because on September 13, 2019 he passed away.

Chapter 10: A Constant Joy

It was 2004 and I was 50 years old. Grandpa had been gone for several years and it was difficult to live in the house where he had lived and died. I needed to get away from Michigan for a while, and I wanted to do something I enjoyed. I missed living in California, so I took a trip there to visit my friend Robert. After my visit, I returned to my Grandpa's old house. I was going through menopause and my emotions were all over the place. It was difficult for me to live in that house that held so many memories of my grandparents, so I sold it and moved to a condo in Fenton.

I was having trouble getting back into work because of my complicated emotional status. Because I wasn't working and I wasn't taking care of Grandpa anymore, I decided to spend more time with my youngest brother, Kenny.

Kenny is my half-brother, but I always simply refer to him as my brother. He was born on April 8, 1971. Due to his mother Sandy's drinking during pregnancy, he was born with fetal alcohol syndrome. He's currently 49 years old but has the IQ of a 5 year, 9-month-old child. Because I was married on April 19, 1969, I never lived with Kenny. It wasn't until November 2, 1992, when I returned to Michigan, that I spent time with him and got to know him. Prior to my return to Michigan, he was living with our dad's sister, Aunt Doris.

Aunt Doris had to eventually place him in Adult Foster Care (AFC) when he was 18 years old because he was aggressive at times and hard for her to handle. My aunt had made plans to move to Florida. Before her departure, she asked me if I would consider being Kenny's guardian. I said I would. It was perfect timing for Kenny because when I contacted Kenny's caseworker, I learned they were about to make him a ward of the state because the home he was currently living in was about to close down. The reason was that after the owner got married and her husband moved in, it was eventually revealed that he was sexually abusing the female mentally challenged clients in the home. I went to court and was granted plenary guardianship on September 9, 1996.

Kenny is a social butterfly and often the life of the party; he's very complimentary to all people. He enjoys helping out with chores. He bowls during the winter months. When I started spending more time with Kenny, I realized what a joy he was to have around. He would always make me laugh. When I first started to have Kenny over for weekend visits, I asked him one time, "What kind of chicken do you like?" He said, "Dead chicken!" When I passed my GED test, he told me that I was as smart as a 2x4. Another time, my son Steve was backing out of the driveway with a truck with a topper on the back, and he asked Kenny if there were any cars coming. Kenny said no. Steve started to back up and somebody honked their horn. Steve said to Kenny, "I thought you said there weren't any cars coming!" Kenny said, "There wasn't. It was a van!" He really has a sense of humor.

Although he loves to kid around, even Kenny can be teased past his limit. On one occasion when he was living with Aunt Doris, our cousin Larry kept on teasing him and wouldn't let up. Finally, when Larry came out of his bedroom, Kenny punched Larry and knocked him right out. Larry didn't tease him after that.

I take care of Kenny two weekends per month. I also take him to see other family members to keep him connected to everyone. He calls our visits his respite care. He always says, "It's nice and quiet here, Linda."

Going forward, a situation had occurred at the AFC where my brother was living in at this time. The owner of the place was misusing Kenny's money. I have always kept a close eye on Kenny's bank account. I had been suspicious of some of the past spending of Kenny's funds, but there was one occasion that didn't make sense at all. The owner had taken everybody in the home to a *free* country concert on Ojibway Island in Saginaw, and she told me that they had all packed lunches and hot chocolate. However, when I got Kenny's resident spending record for the month, there was $40 taken for that weekend.

I called and reported the owner to the Department of Human Services Office of Children and Adult Licensing. They took a report and followed up with a home visit. An investigator showed up at her door, unannounced, at 8 am on a Friday. She was home and definitely caught off guard. She was questioned, found guilty of misusing residents fund, written up, and the information of the report and findings was made available online to the public. Although she wasn't arrested and her facility remained open, I decided to move Kenny because I couldn't trust her.

I decided to have Kenny move into my condo in Fenton. I planned to help him find a job and find him a new medical doctor and psychiatrist. My intention was to start another real estate career in that area, but even if it took me a while to get my first paycheck, Kenny would have social security money coming in to help support him. It sounded like a good plan, but it takes many appointments and a lot of time to get someone with a mental disability established in a new city.

After trying to get Kenny settled for three months, I was still struggling to find time to work. Eventually, I concluded that it was in his best interests to stay in AFC because having him with me affected his medical benefits. I couldn't afford his prescriptions, so I decided to look for an AFC with an opening. Kenny wanted to go back to Bay City so he could go back to the place where he used to work because he liked the familiarity and routine. He also missed going on group activities with other people in the AFC. After realizing how difficult it was to find an AFC that I felt was good enough Kenny, I realized that I should have tried to handle the money situation at the previous AFC a little differently.

I found a home with an opening, but the bad thing about this home was that the woman in charge, Karla, was a friend of the previous AFC owner who had been misusing Kenny's money. Because of this connection, I asked Karla a list of questions I'd written down, but she answered them fully and without hesitation. I talked it over with my brother and he was anxious to get back to Bay City. I called Karla back and told her that we'd like to see the house and which room would be his. We checked it out and agreed to give it a try.

After several months, I realized that I should have waited and found a different home for him. I went to check on him at work one day. His hair was dirty and uncombed and he wasn't shaven. He was carrying his lunch and looked very unhappy and unkept. I wasn't too happy that he wasn't getting help with his grooming. I had taken my camera with me that visit due to my intuition, so I was able to take his picture in case I needed it for any future incidents, and there was another incident.

I got a call from Karla and she told me that Kenny had eaten a whole package of hot dogs himself. She said she knew it was him because he was the only one upstairs at the time. I asked her why was he up there alone, because that was equivalent to leaving a six-year-old to fend for himself. She said she was busy with her own children downstairs. Karla was clearly in the AFC business primarily for the money because she was giving very minimal care to my brother and the other guys there. I wanted to get him out of there as soon as possible. In the meantime, I decided to take my brother to Florida.

My son Steve lived in Florida, and he wanted my help with door-to-door sales for his decorative concrete business, so we decided that while we were there, we could visit Aunt Doris as well. Kenny hadn't seen her for almost five years, and flying on a plane was going to be a new experience for him. I just hoped that he would be okay once we were in the air. I had him sit by the window, and he was fine.

We were there for about 10-12 days. We went to Steve's apartment in Santa Maria Island first, and then drove Kenny to Aunt Doris' house, which was a good hour and a half away from Steve's. The three of us spent the night there. It was nice to spend time with Aunt Doris after we hadn't seen her for so long. She enjoyed having Kenny over again because she really loved Kenny. We were glad we were able to visit with her while we had the chance because, unfortunately, she passed away in 2007.

The vacation was coming to an end, but I couldn't take my brother to Florida without taking him to Disney World. Kenny really enjoyed his time at the amusement park, especially driving the race cars that stay on the track. We went on that ride twice. Now the kiddie roller coaster – that was another story. Kenny sat in the seat next to Steve, and when the ride started going, he got scared. Right then, he looked like a six-year-old. He yelled to Steve, "Don't let me fall out!" He got through the ride, but he made it clear that he wasn't going on that again. I assured him he wouldn't.

The following day, we spent time at the beach building sandcastles. Kenny had never seen the ocean before. He had a lot of new experiences on this vacation. It was nice to spend time with him and see him enjoy himself. Now it was time to go home, back to Michigan. I wasn't looking forward to going back to the cold weather.

We said our goodbyes to Steve and we were on our way. The flight was fine. An announcement was made and we had about 15 more minutes before we were landing. Suddenly Kenny leaned over and said to me, "It's kind of scary out there, isn't it, Linda?" I hoped he wouldn't start panicking then, but he didn't and we had a safe landing.

After being back for a couple of weeks, I decided to go back to Florida. This time I was going to drive myself there. I was really restless and wanted to be in the sun, and menopause was still in control of my emotions. I felt like I had been drifting since the death of my grandpa, still trying to get myself refocused on what I wanted to do now. I stayed with Steve about three weeks. We made some more sales and I enjoyed the sunshine.

During my stay, the caseworker from Department of Human Services was told that I was in Florida. I received a call from her and she told me that because I was in Florida, she was going to start contacting other family members and ask if they would be Kenny's guardian. I said that wouldn't be necessary because I would remain Kenny's guardian. I hadn't moved or put in a change of address, I just went to help Steve get some more sales and enjoy the Florida sunshine. I was allowed to take an extended vacation if I wanted to, and the AFC could still contact me in Florida. I decided to exercise my rights and I fired that caseworker, which made me feel empowered.

A couple of years ago, Kenny was assigned to work with a new job coach named John. Kenny's job was to go to designated locations to deliver newspapers and pick-up old ones, but he needed a job coach to direct him and drive him around. I set up a time to meet with John so I could see who my brother would be working with, and he seemed okay. However, after a short period of time, I noticed changes in Kenny's emotional and physical behavior. Kenny loves to eat, but he suddenly started turning down food that he normally would have taken. He stopped making eye contact with me when we talked. I knew something wasn't right. I suspected that he was being emotionally abused.

One day, he came home with a new jacket, and I asked where he'd gotten it, and he said John had given it to him. John hadn't told anyone about taking Kenny to buy a jacket, which I later found out he'd done during working hours. Kenny also told me that John was taking Kenny over to his house between stops, and this definitely was against the rules. After all of this, John asked me if Kenny could come over for dinner and do other activities with him after work, and when I didn't give him an immediate answer, he became irritated. I told the company everything that had happened, and although I didn't have proof of anything, John was removed from his position with Kenny and offered a position somewhere else in the company, but he declined. I also started taking Kenny to therapy. Within two weeks, the staff noticed that Kenny was back to his old self.

If you have a loved one with a mental disability, you can still tell when something is off. Always know who they are working with and who is taking care of them. After all, they need you to advocate for them. I am still Kenny's guardian, and I plan to be his guardian for as long as I am able to.

Chapter 11: Gone Too Soon

Pam was my youngest sister. Because of my dad's habit of partying while we were growing up, Pam started drinking and smoking from a young age. She was so unhappy growing up that when she was 14 years old, she and a friend hitchhiked all the way to Arizona. She was eventually picked up by the police and the state flew her and the friend back to Michigan.

Pam was married very young also. She was just 16 when she had her first baby, a boy named Jay. She had three more children afterward: Brad, Kari, and Peter. When Peter was born, he wasn't able to get enough oxygen to his brain, and therefore he's severely mentally challenged. He lived at home until his early teens, and then he was placed in an AFC.

Pam gradually became an alcoholic. She decided to pack up her things and leave all four of her children with their father, just like our mom had done to us. It broke my heart, especially because she always wanted a daughter and then chose to leave her behind.

Eventually, Pam met her second husband William who was a mechanic. He was a heavy drug user at one time (things like heroin), but when I knew him, he only drank and smoked pot and cigarettes. Pam finally seemed like she had found happiness in her life.

Eventually, Pam achieved sobriety in 1995, making it much more enjoyable to spend time with her. In April 1996, Pam and I took a trip to Nevada and California because she had never been out there before. Our mother and step-dad, Hutch, were living in Nevada, so we decided to visit them and then fly to California and go to Disneyland together. I really liked Hutch a lot, and this was the first time Pam had met him.

I wanted Pam to see and enjoy as many things as possible during this trip. In Nevada, we went to the casinos in Reno and saw *Splash!* My mom had housekeeping work during the days at Circus Circus casino, so Pam and I would spend the days with Hutch until our mom got home. Hutch drove us to Lake Tahoe, which was incredibly beautiful. The lake was surrounded by the Sierra Nevada and Carson Mountain ranges. The mountain peaks were covered with snow, and the lake's water was so crystal clear that the rocks were visible at the bottom. There were also beautiful beaches all along the shorelines.

After we had enjoyed exploring Nevada and spending time with our mom and step-dad, it was time to catch our flight to California. When we landed in Los Angeles International Airport (LAX), it was very busy. When Pam and I were standing outside the terminal waiting for the shuttle bus to come, there were three lanes of traffic going by in both directions. There were taxi cabs, shuttle and Greyhound buses, limousines, and cars lined up waiting to pick up passengers. Horns were honking constantly and the strong smell of exhaust made Pam and I so sick that we could hardly talk. However, we'd already made plans to go to Disneyland, so we went regardless.

Pam and I had a great time at Disneyland. I will always cherish the memory of our ride on Splash Mountain and the picture of us screaming as we held onto the rollercoaster. On another day, we also went to Knott's Berry Farm and ate some of their famous chicken. This vacation was the most fun we had together during our adult lives, and I will always remember it.

Shortly after Pam and I came back from our vacation, I got a call from Mom. Hutch was getting very confused and disoriented. He had gone into their small bathroom and he couldn't figure out how to get out. My mom had to have a neighbor come over and help him. They set up an appointment to see his doctor and get checked out. The news wasn't good. He had 10-12 cancerous tumors in his head, and the doctor said he had about six months to live. Sadly, he died on August 13, 1996.

After our trip to Nevada and California, Pam stayed out in the country in Midland with her husband William. They were happily married for 10 years and enjoyed spending time with their grandkids. In 2000, William was diagnosed with throat cancer and needed to have major surgery to get a tumor at the back of his throat removed. While he was at home in recovery, he was unable to clear his throat and choked on his phlegm. Pam felt responsible because she wasn't able to save him even though it wasn't her fault. Due to the combination of her emphysema and the stress of William's death, her health began to deteriorate. She sold her home in the country and moved to the city because she needed to be closer to her doctors and the hospital if she needed them.

It was May 2007, and my little sister Pam was doing very poorly. Hospice was coming over to her house and a hospital bed had been set up in her living room. Hospice gave us – her family – devastating news; they thought she'd only live through the weekend. She was only 49 years old. The hospice nurse said that she was their youngest patient. Her chronic obstructive pulmonary disease (COPD), along with the osteoporosis she had from using the steroids in her inhalers, had caused her to have to use liquid morphine for pain and anxiety.

Pam used to enjoy riding motorcycles because her late husband William had a nice Harley. One day when talking with our sister Deborah on the phone, she told me that she knew a group of guys that rode motorcycles and she said she'd call one of them to see if we could make arrangements to take Pam for a final ride. We wanted her to enjoy every minute of life she had left. When the group was on their way, I told Pam that we had a surprise for her. I helped her get dressed, got her into the wheelchair, took her outside, and parked her at the end of the driveway. A few moments later, there were 18 loud motorcycles coming right toward us. They looked like a swarm of bees, and the noise drew the neighbors out of their homes to see what was going on. I told Pam, "This is your surprise; you're going for a ride." Her face lit up with delight. She rode in a sidecar for a half-hour, and she had a big smile on her face when she returned. We were all very grateful that they did this for her.

The weekend was over, and she was still alive, but nobody really knew how much time she had left. I was living in Fenton at the time, which was about an hour away. I stayed with her and took care of her along with Steve and her oldest son Jay. I helped her with bathing, cutting her nails, and washing her hair; the biggest challenge was doing this all quickly before her oxygen levels got too low. It was very stressful.

Steve and Jay took turns sleeping on the couch because Pam would get up at all times of the night. She needed to be assisted to walk to the bathroom either by one of us or with a walker or cane because she was very weak and fragile.

One day while I was taking care of her, I was on the phone, and our mother and Jay were sitting on the couch. Pam got up and started walking. My nephew looked at her and said, "Mom, where's your cane?" He didn't get the words out of his mouth before I suddenly heard a huge crash. My little sister's legs gave out and 80 pounds of her dead weight hit the floor. I was in the other room and went charging into the living room where my sister was lying. We comforted her and called hospice immediately. We didn't want to pick her up just in case she broke something because we might have made things worse. Fortunately, she didn't suffer any major injuries, but I'll never forget that sound.

There were a few times when Pam and I were alone in the house. During one of these times, she asked me if there was anything of hers in particular that I would like to have. I said I'd like to have her clock that chimed because it would remind me of the time we spent together. I always tried my best to express my feelings and how much I loved her, but she was so drugged up that I don't know if what I was saying was making any sense to her. Eventually, I convinced her to let me record our conversation so I could hear her voice even when she was gone. I wrote down some questions, and we went into her bedroom to carry out the conversation.

Six months had gone by and Pam was still alive but slowly losing the desire to live. My eyes had bags and dark circles underneath them; I hadn't been getting proper rest and it had taken a toll on me.

On the morning of December 28, 2007, I got up at 3 or 4 am to use the bathroom. My sister was up, sitting on the edge of her hospital bed. I hugged her and told her that I loved her. Jay informed me that her heart rate was at 200 beats per minute. Hospice was called and came over. We were told she would die sometime that day. She died with her family standing at her bedside, just before 2 pm. I was in total disbelief. It seemed like a bad dream. My little sister was gone. I didn't know until after she has passed that hospice had given my sister the option of taking a pill to increase her heart rate intentionally so that she died of a heart attack rather than of suffocation from her lung disease. My nephew gave her the pill at her request.

There's no good day for a funeral. Pam's was on January 1, 2008. It was not an ideal way to start off the New Year.

I still have the recording of the conversation I had with Pam before she passed away, and I have the clock she gave me, but I haven't yet been able to bring myself to listen to the recording or put batteries in the clock and listen to it chime.

Chapter 12: My Soul Mate Experience

After the loss of my little sister, I decided that I needed to move on and start living my own life. I moved to Midland, which was closer to my family, and rented a house that was just two doors down from where my sister Pam had been living. Steve had been having trouble making sales of his own for his business in Florida, so he moved in with me. My nephew Jay came to live us after a few months as well. I needed some income and I wanted to stay busy, so I did merchandising work and cleaning. At one point in time, I was working three jobs in a given day. I was totally burnt out.

After about a year and a half of living in this overworked state, I decided a visit to California would be a welcome break. I didn't think I should move back there quite yet, but I really missed living there. It was late August 2009 and I had recently been thinking of a friend, a man I'd met in 1979 at the Coldwell Banker real estate office. I tried contacting him and found out he had moved back to Hawaii, but had recently relocated back to California. I found him by calling an ex-roommate, who gave me the number and name of the broker my friend currently worked for. I called the broker and explained who I was and that I was looking for Derek. He said he'd be sure to leave him the message.

Within a couple of days, Derek returned my call. As soon as I answered the phone and heard his voice, I felt an instant connection. It was like we picked up where we left off despite the fact that we'd been out of touch since 1990 – 19 years. He told me that he was just talking about me and a movie we'd seen together years ago. We had a nice conversation and wanted to see one another.

Back in 1980 we'd dated, but quickly realized an intimate relationship wasn't there between us. However, we were still great friends and always had fun. We always laughed a lot when we were together; he has a great laugh, especially after smoking a little marijuana. We loved to go out to lunch and eat Mexican food. We had a lot of things in common – a love of adventure, eating, working out, smoking pot, the ocean, movies, concerts, hiking, meditating, and making money, of course.

I made reservations and went to California in November 2009. Derek met me at the airport and picked me up. He'd changed quite a bit, but so had I. We were both getting older, but to me, that was the only thing that had changed. He was the same Derek I'd always known, and it was great to see him again.

After catching up with each other, we talked about what I wanted to do on my vacation. I told him I wanted to go to the beach, eat some good Mexican food, and listen to some music. He had been wanting to go on a hike but didn't have anybody who was physically able and had the time to go with him. He said the place he wanted to go was in Utah, and I agreed to take the hike with him. I'd flown to California for a vacation and now I was in a rental car heading for Utah. We stayed at a place by Zion National Park. The place was loaded with monks.

Derek got information regarding the different hikes in Utah prior to leaving California, and he chose the most dangerous one. We went to Angel's Landing. It was a 4-hour hike roundtrip. I was fit and confident that I could do it. We started the hike and it gradually was climbing in elevation. The trail had drop offs on both sides with only chain railings between us and a 1,500-foot fall. Eventually, we came to an area where there were more chains strung to help people pull themselves up the mountain because the trail was so steep. I didn't know this hike would be so intense when I'd signed up for it. I reached a point where I was afraid to climb up the rock and continue; I'm really not too fond of heights, so this was really out of my comfort zone. Derek had always liked to push me to try new things, but I knew he would never put me in danger. After looking up and contemplating whether or not to go on, I finally got up the nerve to continue. In the meantime, Derek came back for me. We came to Scout's Lookout, which was a large, flat area where we were able to take in the magnificent view of the mountains of Utah. It was an incredibly freeing, but somewhat scary, feeling to stand up there.

Now we were almost to the end of the hike. The trail dove straight down and then shot straight up to the final lookout point, Angel's Landing. I didn't feel that confident hiking something that steep and standing that high up. I told Derek to go on himself while I stayed put on the landing. He enjoyed the final stretch, but I wanted to stay safe. People had fallen to their deaths hiking to Angel's Landing. It was an incredible experience and I'm very glad that I did it, but if I would have read the description of the hike first, I probably wouldn't have done it.

When we got back to California, I only had two days left of my vacation, and I had another friend who I wanted to see. During the last night with Derek, I felt something emotionally that I couldn't quite identify at the time. I hadn't felt anything like that before. I knew I wasn't in love with him, but there was a very strong spiritual connection; I had never felt so spiritually grounded and happy from within in my life. I gave most of the credit to Derek's lifestyle. He hardly watched TV, and he listened to meditation music when he got up. He ate well and drank water all day long. He was always reading positive articles, walking barefoot in the sand to be close with nature, meditating before bed, and going to bed early. While I was with him, I did all these things as well.

The last day had come, and it was time for me to spend time with my other friend. Derek wasn't happy about me spending time with someone other than him, but neither was I at the time. However, since this was the only day I had left before I went back home to Michigan, I still made arrangements with my friend Robert to meet at a mall.

Derek dropped me off, kissed me on the cheek, and drove away. I started to cry, but I didn't know why. The whole time I was waiting for Robert to show up, I was trying to hold back the tears, but I couldn't – they came rolling down my cheeks under my sunglasses. I wiped my tears when Robert arrived and tried to compose myself. My visit with Robert the next day was short but sweet, and I was glad I was able to catch up with him. Robert drove me to the airport and I returned to my home in Midland.

When I got home, Steve immediately noticed a positive change in me. He told me to try and remember how I felt in that moment so I could stay that way. I was on a natural high.

After my return, Derek and I were emailing one another at least once a day. That trip had been the most memorable vacation I'd had in my life. Three weeks went by and Derek called me, which was unusual. I knew something was up, but I was surprised when I realized he had called to ask me to move in with him. Even though I'd had the same thoughts the past few weeks and was sure that was what I wanted, at that moment, I wasn't able to give him an immediate answer. My whole family lived in Michigan; his lived in Hawaii.

After thinking about his proposal for a month, I decided I would move in with Derek. I always felt so good when we were together, and I wanted to feel like that all the time. I finally told him I would move in with him, and although he said still wanted me to live with him, I could tell his enthusiasm about the idea was gone. I thought that maybe he was hurt that I hadn't agreed immediately when he had asked, but it was huge decision for me to make. I didn't want to leave my family behind again, and I could tell that many of my family members – namely my sister and my mom – didn't want me to leave. I was also still Kenny's guardian, and he would have missed me terribly. Even though I knew all of this, I wanted to hold onto the happiness that I experienced when I was with Derek because it was something that I wasn't able to achieve in Michigan.

I was preparing to move and thinking about how to make an income while out in California. Since I loved working in real estate, I planned to retake the California real estate exam since my license had expired. It was February 2010 and the date for my move was approaching quickly. I'd been checking on airfare prices and found a flight to San Diego for a great price, but would either have to rent a car or have somebody pick me up. Before I bought the ticket, I called Derek to see if he would be able to pick me up on my arrival date, but he didn't answer. I went ahead and bought the ticket because the travel agent could only hold that price until the end of the business day. When Derek returned my call, he was furious that I'd made the reservation without waiting for his approval. Even though I explained to him why I couldn't wait for his response, he was still angry. I've seen him act a little moody at times, but I had never seen him act this controlling before.

Regardless of his irritation, my ticket was already paid for and I would be arriving in California on March 9, 2010. Derek and I still emailed each other in the following weeks, but his anger with me never faded completely. About a week before my flight, I got an email from Derek saying he changed his mind and he didn't want me to live with him. He said he didn't need me. I couldn't believe what I was reading. I was totally devastated and confused. Tears immediately started running down my face, and I felt like there was a hole in my heart where that spiritual connection with Derek had been. I was ready to cancel my plans and stay in Michigan, but Steve encouraged me to move to California anyway. He knew how much I loved the state, and he knew I had other friends there who could help me find a place to live. I agreed with Steve and stuck with my decision to move.

I didn't speak with Derek again until 2014 when I was visiting California. I talked to him the night prior to set up an approximate time to meet. The next morning, Robert gave me a ride, but he ended up stopping at the store to pick up some things, so I called Derek to let him know that I would be about half an hour later than I thought, and he started yelling at me, so I apologized. We didn't even have a specific meeting time set, so I thought he overreacted, but he was still incredibly angry.

We agreed to meet at Starbucks in Aliso Viejo, where Derek lives. It was about 30 minutes south of Long Beach. I went to Starbucks and decided a cup of coffee sounded good, so I sat at an outdoor table and waited for Derek. I was sipping, watching, and waiting anxiously. Finally, I called him and asked where he was. He told me he was at a Starbucks, but obviously not the same one as me. I was at the exact intersection where he told me to meet him, but Starbucks is like 7-11 or McDonalds: there's one on every block.

He finally whipped into the parking lot of the right Starbucks and slammed on his brakes. I approached the car, knowing he was frustrated and angry with me now. That little episode just added fuel to the fire. He told me to follow him to Costco because he wanted to pick up some ingredients for dinner. We went into the store and he wasn't saying much; I felt like I was walking on eggshells. This wasn't what I expected since I hadn't seen him for five years. I followed him back to his place. He carried the groceries in and got dinner started.

While Derek was in the kitchen cooking, I offered to help, but he said, "No, I've got it." I turned to walk away, thinking that I should let him cool off. He finally grabbed me and hugged me, which made me feel a little better, but he was still in a bad mood. This wasn't the kind of hospitality I was expecting, especially after the great time we had during our hike in 2009. Derek was a great cook and made a lot of meals from his Korean and Hawaiian roots, so the dinner he made for us that night was delicious. He made us each a plate and handed mine to me where I was sitting at the kitchen table, then he went into the living room and sat in a chair in front of the TV with his plate.

I asked, "Aren't you going to join me?"

He said, "No."

I didn't know why he was acting this way. I hadn't done anything intentionally to be treated like that, and if this is the way he was going to treat me, I was out of there. I did spend the night there, and he at least gave me his bed and he slept in a sleeping bag on the living room floor. We were soul mates, but we were certainly not lovers.

In the morning, Derek seemed to be in a better mood. We were sipping hot cups of coffee, and then Derek started talking about some ideas he had for the rest of my vacation. I immediately knew that I was going to tell him no because I did not want him to take control of my entire vacation like he had done in 2009. I had excluded seeing other people and doing other things to take that hike, but this time, I had my own plans that worked for me with the budget I had for the trip.

Derek is by far the most intuitive person I've ever met. He started throwing out different suggestions that all included hiking and doing what he wanted to do, but he sensed the resistance from me and called me on it. He got mad that I wasn't interested in reshaping my entire agenda just for him.

He took another route and decided he'd like me to see a condo he'd bought that he wanted to flip. And while we were there, he thought I would help him clean some windows and sweep off the patio. I told him that I didn't want to cook or clean. I thought that he should Google the word "vacation" because I'm pretty sure those activities aren't part of the definition. He was getting more frustrated with me because I wouldn't allow him to control me. At this point in my life, I had enough experience with emotional abuse to recognize the red flags.

We were getting nowhere, and I decided I wasn't going to waste any more of that beautiful California day, so I went off to the pool and let him do what he wanted. While I was laying by the pool, I knew I had to leave. I came inside about an hour and a half later, showered, and packed up all of my things because I planned to go back to Long Beach. Derek was being emotionally abusive and I wouldn't take it anymore. When Derek came in to talk to me, I knew that he saw my packed bags, which were openly visible.

Derek had previously asked me if I'd take him to pick up his car from the repair shop in the morning when it was ready, and I had told him that I would.

We were drinking our morning coffee and then he turned to me and said, "I think you should leave."

He knew I was already planning to leave, but I know him. He wanted to feel like it was his decision and he was in control. I recognized this, but I didn't say anything. I let him think he was in control. I grabbed my suitcase by the handle and pulled it with firmness and intention and we drove to the repair shop. I turned off my car because I planned to wait until he knew his car was ready before I left. He grabbed the keys from my ignition and threw them at me, calling me a bitch.

Then, he picked up the keys and put them in his pocket so I wasn't able to leave until he gave them back. I didn't know what his issue was with me anymore, but I knew I didn't deserve that treatment, so once he had his car and gave me the keys back, I left.

I believe what happened was that Derek ignored his intuition. He said I kept popping up in his mind weeks before I came to California, but he didn't contact me until the week before I was going to leave, so I already had plans made. If he had listened to his gut and hadn't waited as long to call, maybe we would have been able to make plans and spend more time together. Regardless of this, it wasn't my fault. We should have been able to laugh off the Starbuck mix up, but he let it ruin our entire visit.

I still believe that Derek and I had a special soul mate connection that was unexplainable, which he recognized long before I did. I will find myself thinking about him frequently and feel that he is thinking about me at the same time because I can feel his energy. It's a shame that we no longer enjoy one another's company because of his stubbornness and short temper. A soul mate relationship happens but once in a lifetime if you're lucky, but I refuse to tolerate any abuse to maintain that relationship. I haven't heard from him since 2014, and I don't know if we'll ever speak again, but I know for certain that after seeing his abusive side for the first time, I'm glad that I didn't move in with him back in 2010.

Chapter 13: Great Actor

Back in March of 2010, I had already planned to move to California with Derek. When he backed out at the last minute, I moved to California anyway. I had already said my goodbyes to my family, or tried to. When I went to my mother's apartment to tell her goodbye, she wouldn't answer the door.

I managed to get a ride from San Diego to Long Beach. My friend Robert owned a one-story house that he had divided into three separate apartments. One of the apartments was vacant, so he let me stay there. It didn't take me too long to clean up and settle in; all I had was what I could fit into two suitcases: no furniture, no bed, no car – nothing. Just clothing and a few personal items.

Robert lived in the back apartment, and a single man named Thomas lived in the studio apartment between Robert and me. Immediately upon being introduced to Thomas, I could see that he was interested in me, and I was attracted to him as well. He was a small Hispanic man who had a big smile and raised his eyebrows when he looked at me.

While I was living there, Robert invited the two of us over to a friend's house for happy hour. At the party, Thomas and I had a few drinks, some food, and danced. Thomas happened to be a great dancer, and I enjoy dancing also, so we danced the night away to the point that Thomas' legs were sore the next day, but we had a lot of fun.

Thomas knew I didn't have much of anything, so when he cooked for himself, he made enough for me also and would invite me over for dinner. We shared a patio area where we could sit in the morning sun, and Thomas and I would go out there with our cups of coffee and talk. He was easy to talk to.

Even at a reduced rate, the place I was renting was more than I could afford. Robert thought I should consider a roommate, so he ran some ads for me. He would interview potential roommates before he would let me meet them to make sure that I felt comfortable and safe with the person. Eventually I ended up with a male roommate. It worked out well because he was on the road a lot for work, but he still paid half of the expenses and brought things to the household that I didn't have.

In the meantime, Thomas and I were spending time together pretty much every day and getting to know each other. After only two weeks of knowing him, he asked me to marry him. I knew that that was a bit of a red flag, but I was still flattered. I said no because it was way too soon and I didn't know him very well yet. My rejection didn't faze Thomas, and he continued to pursue me. He didn't have a car because his license had been suspended since he wasn't paying his back-child support for his kids from a previous marriage, but that didn't stop him from walking to pick up dinner for both of us.

It was a beautiful day in sunny Southern California, and it happened to be my birthday. I had invited a handful of people to come over later that evening to celebrate. There was food, beer, wine, and of course, cake and ice cream. The people showed up, and I was having a wonderful time socializing with old and new friends. When my guests were ready to light the candles on my cake and sing "Happy Birthday," everybody gathered in the kitchen, except Thomas. No one knew where had he gone, so I ended having to leave my party to go find him. I looked around the block, but I didn't see him anywhere, so I just went back home and continued without him. I was irritated that he chose to leave the party at that moment. He had obviously done it for attention to take the focus away from me, and I knew that was another red flag in our relationship. Eventually he came back, and when we asked him where he had been, he said he went to the store. He seemed sincerely sorry for treating me that way, and I forgave him and pretended that I hadn't noticed his narcissistic behavior.

Thomas continued to pursue me; he had been alone for a long time, and so had I. While on the treadmill at the gym, where I do my best thinking, I thought to myself, "He really does seem to love me. Why shouldn't I marry him?" When I got back from the gym, I showered and got ready to eat dinner with Thomas.

After dinner, I said, "Aren't you going to ask me again?"

He asked me to marry him one more time, and this time, I said yes. Thomas was so excited that he picked up the phone and called everybody he could think of. I told Robert, and he wasn't happy at all because he thought I was moving too fast; he warned me that Thomas was an alcoholic and that our relationship would not be a healthy one, but I thought he was just being overprotective. Thomas drank a lot, but he claimed he wasn't an alcoholic.

Despite Robert's warning, Thomas and I decided that we wanted to go look at wedding rings. We went to JCPenney, where I had a store credit card and found a set of rings that we liked. Thomas said if we used my credit card to get the rings, he'd pay me back when he got his Social Security check on the third of the month. I knew his narcissistic behavior was showing again, but I once again ignored the red flag. I was so excited to be shopping for my wedding ring that I didn't mind if I had to buy it myself for the time being.

Thomas' adult daughters from his previous marriage made plans to celebrate at a local Mexican restaurant. I met his three daughters and one son. He also had one grandson with his girlfriend there. We ate a delicious meal, and Thomas' daughters brought a white cake with raspberry filling. His family was very nice, and they liked and accepted me. Thomas had been alone for so long that they were happy he'd finally met somebody. His mother was the only one who didn't seem happy that we were getting married; it was almost as if she knew our relationship wouldn't last. One day we were listening to the radio and a song by Etta James came on. The name of the song was "At Last." We decided right then that would be our song.

After I agreed to marry Thomas, he said that to show how much he loved me, he would let me handle all of his finances after he cashed his Social Security check. The only recreational expenses he said he needed were his cigarettes and occasional beer. I had always worked my whole life and took care of myself, so budgeting money for someone else and having him take care of me was a welcome break. I took this gesture as a sign of Thomas' love and trust, which is incredibly important in any relationship.

Thomas and I decided to get married on July 14, 2010. We just wanted to have a courthouse wedding with witnesses. The courthouse was in Norwalk, California. We went there to start the paperwork and look at the room they used for the ceremony. It was a big room with an archway decorated with flowers, which was much more than I expected. After our paperwork was completed, Thomas informed me that the date we chose was the same as the date that he had married his ex-wife. I had no clue, and I hadn't thought about asking. After I found out, I told him I would prefer if we changed it, but he refused and said it would be easier to leave things the way they were. I was seeing another red flag of power and control, but the plans were already in place.

The courthouse was extremely busy that day. We were scheduled to be married at 1 pm, but they weren't ready for us until 4:20 pm. They finally called our names, so we walked into the ceremony room. A local judge officiated our wedding;

I was pretty teary-eyed when we were exchanging our vows. It was a short, simple ceremony, but very emotional. Thomas and I and our two witnesses, one of Thomas' sisters and her boyfriend, went to El Torito restaurant for dinner and drinks. We toasted in celebration of our marriage and went home as a married couple.

Since we had gotten married so quickly, Thomas had yet to meet my family. He was born and raised in California, and he hadn't even been out of the state before, so in September of 2010, we decided to take a trip to Michigan. I was looking forward to seeing my family even though I'd only been gone for six months. While I was gone, Steve and Jay, whom I was sharing a home with prior to going to California, had moved to Beaverton, Michigan where they were both employed, and they had moved all of my possessions with them. Beaverton was a pretty resort town, so the population was seasonal.

The home my son and nephew were renting was located right behind a convenience store/gas station. There was also a restaurant across the street. The best part about the house was the lake view from the living room window. It was a manufactured home with three bedrooms, two full bathrooms, and a full basement with high ceilings. Light bulbs went off in my head once I saw that basement; it was a perfect place to grow marijuana. There wasn't any place at the house I was renting in California to grow inside or out. However, I'd just moved back to California for the second time, and I wasn't feeling ready to return permanently back to Michigan. Thomas, on the other hand, really liked Michigan and wanted to move right then. It was September and winter would be coming soon; this would be the time of year to be in California, so I told him I didn't want to move.

While visiting, Thomas and I stayed at the house by ourselves because Steve was staying with his girlfriend pretty frequently and Jay had gone to stay with his sister. Before he left, Jay told Thomas that there was whiskey in the cupboard and he could help himself if he wanted some. Thomas took advantage of that offer and drank the whole bottle, which had been nearly full. I knew that that was a sign of Thomas' alcoholism, which Robert had warned me about, but I just told myself we were on vacation. Still, I thought he could have left Jay with some. We stayed in Michigan for about a week, and we had a good visit. Thomas liked my mom and the rest of my family, and they seemed to like him, too.

After we returned home, Thomas and I settled into a routine as a married couple does. In the evening, Thomas and I used to sit on the front porch. I would smoke marijuana, and Thomas would smoke cigarettes and drink beer. One day, while I was work, he started drinking earlier than usual. By the time I got home at 4 pm, he was already so drunk that he had fallen on the porch and hit his head. I knew that head injuries could lead to serious problems, so I called Robert and asked him if he'd help me get Thomas to the ER. Robert helped me get Thomas into a sitting position, but Thomas refused to go to the ER. I knew reasoning with drunk people is difficult, but I was concerned because he had already gotten one head injury from drinking in the past. I was starting to wonder what kind of relationship had I gotten myself into.

One weekend when I was home with Thomas and my roommate, I heard the two of them arguing. I knew Thomas had started it over something insignificant. His red flags kept popping up now, and it was getting harder for me to ignore them. Thomas was clearly an actor and could find almost anything to argue about. Robert, my landlord and friend, came over to talk to Thomas and me. I felt like I was getting scolded for my husband's behavior, almost like he was my child instead of my husband. I had addressed Thomas' drinking habits prior to our marriage, and he had assured me that his drinking wasn't out of control nor would it become so. I was foolish in love at the time, so I chose to believe him, which I now know was a mistake.

Despite his drinking, Thomas was incredibly intuitive, which I found amazing, but also scary. One day, he looked at me and told me exactly what it was that I was thinking, and he was spot on. I felt like my head was transparent, and I became more conscious of what I was thinking around him because I didn't want Thomas to see anything he didn't like. At this point, I saw another red flag; through his intuition, Thomas was controlling my thoughts.

The old BMW I had been driving died after I had it for only four months, and I needed a new car so I could do my merchandising work. My mechanic said he had a 1989 red convertible BMW for sale. I'd always wanted a red car. I wasn't thrilled that the car was a convertible, but I didn't have a lot of options or money. It was nice and I ended up buying it. My part-time merchandising work brought in $10 an hour. I wasn't going to get anywhere with a part-time job with such a low wage. I kept thinking about the opportunity of growing marijuana in the basement in Michigan, so I told Thomas in October or November that I would be ready to go back to Michigan. Once I had changed my mind, he changed his back and decided he didn't want to leave. The red flags were becoming clearer every day. I saw now that Thomas was all about power and control, but I had been ignoring it this whole time.

Thomas finally agreed to move to Michigan in January 2011. We were going to fly, so that meant I needed to sell the red BMW. When I had still been driving my first BMW, a man had put a note on my windshield and said to call him if I ever decided to sell the car. I kept the note even though my first BMW had died because I figured he might be interested in old BMWs. I called him to ask if he was interested in the red

BMW I had, and he was. He looked it over and really liked it, but couldn't buy it that day, so he said he would get back to me.

Meanwhile, Thomas and I knew we weren't leaving until January 6, so rather than paying prorated rent for six days at the Long Beach apartment, one of Thomas' sisters let us stay with her for a week.

We wanted to keep most of our things in California since we were flying to Michigan. I also wanted to make sure Thomas wanted to stay in Michigan before we decided what to do with our furniture. Thomas had a niece that lived nearby his sister's house. She was a single mom, and she had an empty garage that she let us use for storage. We agreed to pay her $50 per month to hold our things in California. We also agreed to pay an extra $50 per month to store the red BMW if we didn't sell it. She didn't have room for the car, but her mother did, and said we could park it there, but she would give her daughter the money. Her daughter needed the extra money, and our things would be in a safe place. However, I wasn't thrilled about the idea because I have had bad experiences when relying on family members.

We got everything packed up, rented a small U-Haul, and moved it to the garage. While we stayed there, we ate meals together and everything seemed to be going just fine. That is, until December 31, 2010.

It was New Year's Eve. I was excited, looking forward to 2011 with new adventures on my horizon. It was a nice sunny day in Southern California, and I was sitting outside in a lawn chair taking it all in because I knew when we got to Michigan, there would probably be snow on the ground.

At about 1-2 pm, Thomas decided he was going to have a drink to celebrate 2011. This was a pretty early start for Thomas, but he wasn't intolerable when he was just drinking beer. I enjoy watching the New Year's Eve countdown on

TV, and so did his family. Thomas kept slipping away so we wouldn't see him drinking, so I lost track of him several times. It got to be midnight and I was looking forward to getting my New Year's kiss from my new husband, but he was nowhere in sight. I noticed the red flag again, just like I had noticed at my birthday party.

I found him out in the garage, completely drunk. His brother-in-law had given Thomas a bottle of whiskey. I hated when Thomas drank whiskey because his demeanor completely shifted and he became incredibly mean. I had noticed the red flag of Thomas' alcoholism before, but I couldn't ignore it anymore. I knew now that I'd married a full-blown alcoholic who had played me. I was mad at myself for ignoring the signs for so long, and I was disappointed with Thomas. He was the one who had wanted to marry me so badly, but he clearly didn't love me as much as pretended he did.

After the disappointment of being left alone at midnight of the New Year, I decided I might as well go to bed. A little while later, I was startled awake by a growling noise, and I thought a wild animal had gotten into my room. When I sat up to see what it was, I realized that it was Thomas. He was sitting in a chair in the bedroom, growling like an animal. I got up and tried to get him to go to bed. He refused and continued to growl. After a few minutes, he muttered that he felt like killing somebody. I was terrified when I heard that; I'd never seen him like this. I put on my robe and got my purse and car keys. My hands were shaking so badly, it took me a few moments just to get my car door unlocked. I stayed in the car for a while, scared of being in the same room as him and hoping he would fall asleep soon. After about an hour, I reluctantly went back in and saw that Thomas' nephew was up. When I told him what had happened, he didn't seem surprised; evidently this wasn't the first time.

The next day, Thomas acted as if nothing had happened; I wasn't sure if he even remembered. I convinced myself that Thomas had just overindulged because he was leaving his home state and family soon. I thought that once we were in Michigan, in my home state, things would be better.

It was January 5, 2011, and we were leaving on an early flight to Michigan the next morning. During the day, I received a call from the guy who had looked at my car a couple of weeks before, and he told me that wanted to buy it. I was happy because I'd have some more money to go home with and I'd have one less thing to be concerned about.

When we told my in-laws that we would be selling the red BMW, they were furious. They told Thomas that they had been planning on driving the car until I sold it, and they accused me of knowing that the car was going to sell before I agreed to give Thomas' niece and extra $50 per month to store it. Because they assumed all of these things, I was called a liar even though I didn't lie about anything.

After that incident, their attitude toward me changed, and they told Thomas that we'd have to find another way to get to the airport because they weren't taking us. Regardless of their childish behavior, I'm glad I sold the car. I wasn't going to pay them $50 per month to rack up miles on the car I was trying to sell. I wasn't very optimistic about my relationship with Thomas' family anymore. We called a cab.

Our flight arrived at the Flint Bishop Airport in Michigan, and my son Steve picked us up. We were cramped into a small Chevy S10 pickup truck because that was the only vehicle he had, but we managed. The drive was about an hour-and a-half long, and then we finally arrived at the first home we would share as newlyweds.

The house in Beaverton felt like home to me because all of my belongings were already there. It wasn't until I had lived there for a few months that I realized the safety of the neighborhood was questionable. Steve had moved out to live with his girlfriend, and Jay had moved in with his sister temporarily while he looked for his own place, so Thomas and I had the house to ourselves. When we got married and Thomas asked me to be in charge of his finances, I had made the decision to be financially dependent on him, and he had encouraged this. This was not the norm for me, and I didn't feel comfortable asking him for money. I've worked my whole life and always earned my own money.

After several months of our married life in Michigan, things seemed to be going okay, but they were getting progressively worse. Sometime in late spring, I was taking a shower and when I got out, Thomas was gone. He had refused to get a license even though he received notice that he was eligible to get one, and my car was parked in the driveway, so I thought maybe he was down by the lake. A couple hours later, my neighbor came home and I saw Thomas get out of his car. He hadn't let me know he was leaving, and I asked where they'd gone.

Thomas said they had gone to a local bank where Thomas decided to open a checking account with direct deposit. Upon further discussion, I found out that the account was only in his name and he was only getting one debit card. I wasn't even listed as a beneficiary. Another red flag showed its ugly face; Thomas wanted to take back control of the money after he had specifically asked me to take care of his finances.

I was trying to get everything set up so that I could start growing medical marijuana, which is one of the main reasons why I wanted to move back to Michigan. I had taken classes at Oaksterdam University when I was in California about growing marijuana, opening and running a dispensary, cooking with marijuana, and running a delivery business. I received a certification that I had passed the tests for these classes. With these classes and with my prior experience growing in Northern California, I thought that I would be able to make a good profit growing in Michigan. However, while I was getting everything started, Thomas didn't want me to get another job; he wanted me to remain completely reliant on him.

As more time went by, I started seeing red flags daily. He was not only trying to control me, but was also becoming very emotionally abusive. I would cook dinner, and when I told him it was ready, he would just say, "I'm going to have another cigarette," and go outside to smoke. I would get irritated and tell him he could eat his dinner cold, and then I'd sit down to eat all alone.

Since we moved to Michigan, he was drinking daily. He would start at 4 pm, the beginning of what he would call "happy hour." I had told Thomas that I didn't like how his demeanor changed when he drank whiskey, and he had agreed not to drink it anymore. On one summer day, Thomas walked over to the local store – there were two within walking distance. One sold whiskey and the other only sold beer. I watched out the living room window to see which store he would choose, and I saw him walk to the store that sold whiskey. When he got home, I looked out the back window and saw him put a small brown bag under the porch. I hurried up and scooted into the living room and sat down, knowing that he had hid his whiskey there. I waited for my opportunity to go confirm my suspicions.

A few hours later, he went to take a shower. I went outside, saw the bag, and looked inside. Sure enough, it was whiskey. I had tried talking to him about his drinking habits, but his lies showed me that he thought I was gullible, so I decided to take matters into my own hands. I grabbed the whiskey, hurried back into the house, and hid the bottle in my closet where I knew he wouldn't look for it. He got out of the shower, and we were watching some TV when I decided to ask him what he got from the store, but he didn't admit to buying any whiskey. I didn't press him anymore, and I just waited to see what would happen when he went to look for it later.

At about 10 pm, I told him I was going to bed. I left the bedroom door open because I knew that as soon as he thought I was asleep, he'd go after his whiskey. At 11 pm, the news was broadcasting storm warnings and high wind advisories, so it was not a good time to be going outside. This didn't stop Thomas, and he wasn't going to wait any longer. I glanced into the living room and saw him head toward the back door. I snuck out of bed and peeked around the corner to make sure he was outside. My initial plan had been to open the door and ask him what he was doing out there, but as I approached the door, I changed my mind and blasted the porch light on him as I swung the door open.

He was flat on the ground looking desperately for the bottle he knew he'd hidden there.

I calmly said, "What are you doing out there?"

He said, "I went out to have a cigarette and my lighter fell out of my pocket, and I'm looking for it."

I replied that he shouldn't be out right then because the winds were so strong that they had woken me up, so we both went back into the house and I went back to bed. When I got into bed, I had to put my pillow over my face because I was laughing so hard. He looked around the inside of the house for about three hours before he finally went to sleep in the guest room. He hardly slept with me anymore, even though we'd been married less than a year. His love affair was with his alcohol, and he always put that first.

The next day, I waited to see if Thomas was going to say anything to me about the whiskey, but I doubted he would because I knew he didn't want to admit to buying it, so I decided to tell him I had taken it.

We were sitting at opposite ends of the couch, and I looked right at him and said, "Thomas, I have your whiskey."

If looks could kill, I saw daggers in his eyes. I told him about it because I wanted to show him that he wasn't smarter than me. I gave him back his whiskey, and he drank all of it. He got drunk very quickly, and he was so angry with me that he took a wooden chair and lodged it under the doorknob of the guest bedroom so I couldn't get in.

There were several more occasions when Thomas secretly bought whiskey and thought he had successfully hidden it from me. One day, when I kept finding whiskey in his typical hiding places in the guest bedroom – under the mattress, in his coat pocket, in his boots – I decided to look through my kitchen pantry and see if I could replace the whiskey with something. Apple cider vinegar looks almost identical to whiskey. I carefully poured the whiskey into a separate container, and then poured an equal amount of apple cider vinegar into his whiskey bottle and put the bottle back where I found it.

After dinner, he headed for the whiskey. He got it out, took a big drink, and immediately spat it out all over the bedroom wall. He came out and was actually laughing. He said, "Okay, you got me." I did it a second time a week later and he said, "You got me again." The third time, he got angry, and I knew I had made my point. Although he had laughed it off the first two times, and even I thought his initial reaction was funny, his alcoholism wasn't a joke. I was getting too old to play games and I refused to live with anybody who was going to abuse me.

After a year and seven months of this abusive and neglectful marriage, I'd had enough. I couldn't live like I had been anymore. Thomas wouldn't eat with me, sleep with me, or allow me to do anything without his money or permission. If anyone came over to visit, even my own family, he made them uncomfortable so they wouldn't want to come back. He kept me living in fear. I was afraid of his demeanor when he drank whiskey, I never knew where he was or what he was doing, and I never knew if I would be allowed to have money when I needed it. I hadn't expected to be left alone even while married. When I concluded that I was miserable living like this, I confronted him.

I told him, "You have got to go."

He heard the conviction and authority in my voice and responded, "You mean it, don't you?"

I said I did, and he knew I was serious. I called my travel agent to price a one-way ticket back to California. Thomas called his family and filled them in. I eavesdropped and heard him telling them lies to make it seem like I was the reason our marriage wasn't working out. Among his lies, he told his family, "She's nothing but a pothead." Those words hurt, but I didn't care – I just wanted him gone. He made the necessary arrangements to get picked up from the airport and have a place to stay.

I took him to the airport on February 12, 2012, two days before Valentine's Day. We said our goodbyes, and when I turned and walked away, I felt the tears running down my cheeks. I felt betrayed by him. I had fallen in love with the sober Thomas in California, and I refused to live with anyone who thought they could abuse me and get away with it. After he got to California, he called me several times a week when he was drunk, saying that he still wanted to be together.

After I was separated from Thomas, I emotionally felt like damaged merchandise. I had already been through one abusive relationship with my ex-boyfriend Ray, and even though Thomas didn't physically abuse me like Ray had, the emotional abuse I experienced with Thomas was even more damaging. I decided to reach out to get some moral support, and I found a woman's support group that had meetings once a week for no charge, which I was grateful for because I still had no income.

I attended several meetings, and after a minimum requirement of five meetings, they gave me a free workbook called "Healing the Trauma of Abuse." I was very serious about working on myself because I didn't like my old self. I had allowed myself to become dependent on a man and remain unemployed for longer than I ever had in my life. He had kept me socially isolated and kept my self-esteem so low that I felt socially and emotionally inadequate. I should have known better from my past experiences, so I was angry at myself for letting this happen. After a few meetings, I realized that the women coming to these meetings just kept repeating why they were there, and no one was working toward a solution. I thought that the workbook would help, but by the time everyone in the group had taken their turn sharing, the meetings were almost over, so we never were able to get into the workbook.

I decided to drop out of the group and do the workbook one-on-one with a counselor. The group wasn't all bad, and I did learn from it, but it just didn't fit my needs. One of the best things I got from one of the group meetings was a book recommendation. The name of the book is *Why Does He Do That?* by Lundy Bancroft. After I read the book, my eyes were opened up to what emotional and mental abuse looked like. It was brought to my attention that emotional abuse can have longer lasting negative impacts than even physical abuse. After I finished the book, I made a list of ways that Thomas had been emotionally abusive. I came up with about 30 different things:

- He told me the skin under my neck was wrinkled and saggy.
- He called me a whore.
- He called me a pothead and worm which was lower than dirt.
- His needs always came first.
- He would only buy booze, cigarettes, and snacks for himself when he went to the store.
- He never showed appreciation for my cooking, but always boasted about his own.
- He would barricade himself in the guest bedroom so he could drink.
- He told me I was the reason he was an alcoholic.
- He never looked at me when he talked to me.
- Our one Valentine's Day together, the only thing he gave me was an unsigned convenience store card still in its cellophane.
- On our wedding anniversary, he told me he couldn't afford to take us out to dinner because I had spent his money on cleaning supplies.
- He never told me he loved me after we were married.
- He would never spend time with me, even though he spent plenty of time drinking with our neighbor.
- He rarely slept with me, and when he wanted to, he would be so drunk I didn't want to be near him.

- He'd make sexual comments about other women and compliment their looks without ever giving me the same attention.

- One time, he wanted me to perform oral sex on him when he wasn't clean.

- Another time, he was performing oral sex on me, and I told him to stop, but he held my legs down and continued anyway.

- I had no access to any money.

- I couldn't talk to anybody, not even my own family, without him being jealous.

- He terrorized me by leaving the doors to the house wide open and then he would leave, telling me that he did it so our creepy neighbor could come in and have sex with me.

- He kept all the bedroom and bathroom doors in the house closed so that I never knew where he was.

- He would get my hopes up for something exciting, and then refuse to follow through.

- He would sabotage every occasion that should have been happy.

- Grocery shopping was our only outing, and we had to be back by 4 pm so he could drink.

- He tried to dictate to me who I could keep as my friends.

- He didn't let me drive after dark.

- He wouldn't answer the landline when he knew someone was calling me.

- He would throw his cigarette butts on the ground and ignore the ashtray I had set out for him.

- He invaded my privacy by reading through my private journals that I kept, and then lied about it by saying he was looking for pictures.

- He terrorized me by telling me that I needed to get a gun for my protection because I was going to be murdered.

I included this list in a letter that I sent to Thomas, and I copied it for myself as a reminder for why I got rid of him. A couple weeks after I had sent the letter, I came home to a message on my answering machine from Thomas.

In the message, he said, "I'm sorry, I'm so sorry…for the way you think about me." I had thought I was getting a sincere apology, but he twisted it to make it seem as if my feelings toward him were to blame. My letter hadn't been about my actions, it was about the things that he had done to me. I called him back to confront him. After I told him that I knew he had been emotionally abusing me during our entire relationship.

He had the audacity to say, "I see you've been doing your homework."

I told him, "Yes, that's why you're there, and I'm here."

After he said that, I slammed down the phone and uttered some choice words to myself, then cried. He had known he was abusing me this whole time, and he didn't feel an ounce of remorse.

After that conversation, I filed for divorce. The women's shelter assisted me and provided me with the forms I needed, and I didn't have to pay an attorney since I was a part of the organization. When Thomas got the notice of divorce proceeding, he called me and said that he didn't want this to happen. He thought that because he left me with no money and no income, I would eventually reunite with him in California. He clearly didn't know me at all. I've been surviving on my own my whole life, and I would bounce back; I always have. All I asked for in the divorce was $400 for internet service so I could start my merchandising job again, get an oil change, and have some gas money.

By September 11, 2012, my divorce was final. I didn't miss Thomas, and I actually felt relieved. I didn't have to come home to a drunk husband and I was in full charge of my life once again. He called a few times after that, but I never answered or returned his calls. After a few weeks, he finally stopped calling, and I never heard from him again. It was time for me to move on. I'd learned a very valuable lesson about emotional abuse from my relationship with Thomas, and I definitely know, without a doubt, that I did the right thing by divorcing him.

In December 2016, four years after I had divorced Thomas, I was looking through my mail and saw a letter that was from Thomas' pension company. The letter was asking me to choose a new PIN number for the account. I knew in that moment that Thomas must be dead because he had listed me as his beneficiary while we were married.

I immediately called the pension company and confirmed that Thomas was deceased. Even though Thomas' had been abusive and neglectful, I was caught off guard and became very emotional at the news of his death. I had fond memories of my relationship with the sober Thomas. When I finally received the death certificate, it said the cause of death was cardiac arrest and diabetes mellitus type II. I had known he was diabetic, but I also knew he didn't take care of himself. It was most likely the alcohol that killed him.

Thomas had died on July 12, 2015, two days before our wedding anniversary. Thomas had been deceased for almost 18 months before I found out. Initially, I thought that Thomas might have left his pension to me because he still loved me, but after thinking about how much he had changed during our marriage, I felt that the only reason he left it to me was to taunt me with those monthly payments so I wouldn't forget him. He didn't love me. When you truly love somebody, you don't abuse them.

Chapter 14: Alcoholic Crutch

My brother Crockett was the third baby born. His real name was David Allen, and he shared his first name with our father and grandfather, but was called Davy Crockett for a while, which eventually just became Crockett. I learned later on that he never liked being called Crockett, but he just got used to it and started answering to it.

Once my sister Deborah and I were married and out of the house, Crockett and Pam were left to fend for themselves. As I mentioned earlier, food was scarce, so Pam and Crockett would walk to a nearby grocery store and dumpster dive for whatever food they could find. It made me feel guilty for not being there to continue to take care of them, but I had a tough enough time looking out for myself.

Crockett became a father when he was a teenager in high school, so he never graduated. After having his first two children, Dawn and Tod, Crockett married his girlfriend, Myndi, and they had another daughter named Sonya. Crockett was an excellent mechanic and carpenter, but he was never able to become certified in either field because of his alcoholism. He made his living as a backyard mechanic and carpenter, never really got paid for what his work was worth. After 20 years of marriage and after the three kids were moved out of the house, Crockett and Myndi got a divorce, and he never remarried.

When I moved to Beaverton with Thomas in January 2011, I was exactly ten miles from Crockett's house. My brother had COPD, like our sister Pam and our grandpa had, and he didn't have a driver's license because he was an alcoholic, and he told me that he didn't trust his willpower to resist driving under the influence. For someone who was about only 5'5" and weighed 118 pounds, Crockett sure could drink. He drank three 30-packs of beer per week; that's more than a dozen beers per day.

Our cousin Candy moved in with Crockett to help him with living expenses, cooking, cleaning, and running errands since he couldn't drive. When Crockett's health started deteriorating, I would step in for Candy while she was at work and give Crockett a hand with whatever he needed. Whenever we went to go see his lung doctor, and the doctor told us both that Crockett's lungs were "very, very bad," but he didn't give any further explanation or information in front of me. My brother had quit smoking four years ago when he had seen how sick it had made our little sister Pam, but the damage had already been done. Crockett knew that he wasn't doing well, so he asked his daughter, Dawn, to take care of his funeral arrangements, but she declined, so he asked me instead, and I told him I would. I was hesitant because I had a feeling that Dawn was going to be a problem down the road, but I still thought it was the right thing to do in the moment.

Crockett lost his balance one day and fell while he was home alone, and he wasn't able to get back up. It took his son, Tod, hours to find him. He was taken to the Midland Hospital, where he stayed for a few days. Jay had come to see Crockett, and while Jay, was in the room with him, the doctor told Crockett that he didn't have much longer to live, and Jay finally got to hear why. I was on my way up to the room when Jay came into the hallway and told me that besides the COPD – which we all knew about – Crockett also had lung and bone cancer. This explained why he was getting so thin and weak. Crockett had known about his cancer for at least a few months if not longer, but he didn't tell anybody because he didn't want anyone to feel sorry for him. Even though he was an alcoholic, he still had a lot of pride.

After the truth about his cancer was revealed, he lifted his shirt and said, "Look, I look like a starving deer." He had no body fat, and his ribs were clearly visible.

Before Crockett left the hospital, he was being given morphine, and he continued to take it once he returned home. Jay and Candy stayed with Crockett and took turns watching over him. Hospice came over to discuss the medication administration and schedule. My mom, Dawn, Sonya, Jay, Candy, and I were all present, and Jay and Candy kept Crockett's medication diary since they were his caregivers.

After Crockett got home from the hospital, I went over to see him. Before I went in, Jay told me that he was very, very stoned. A friend of Crockett's had made some pudding with marijuana in it. A normal serving would have been one tablespoon, and that would have been enough to get him high, but Crockett had eaten 14 tablespoons, plus he was still on liquid morphine. He knew that he was dying, and he was scared. I had never seen anybody look so stoned in my whole life. His hazel eyes were wide open and glassy looking. He stared without blinking, and he looked empty, like his soul had already left his body. It was a look that I'll never forget.

On April 21, 2012, Jay called and said Crockett wasn't breathing well. His breathing had been getting more and more labored since that morning, so Jay suggested that I get our mom and sisters over to say our goodbyes because it wouldn't be much longer before he died. Once we got there, everybody took their turn and went and whispered in his ear. We let him know that we were there for him and loved him. All the while, I was holding Crockett's small hand. By 9:50 pm that evening, he died. For a brief period of time, the room went silent. Then all of a sudden, Dawn started wailing and put her arms straight out to a few different people, wanting somebody to comfort her, but nobody did. I think they were still in shock, just as I was. I got up and embraced her as we cried together. I was in disbelief; it seemed like a bad dream. Nobody knew what to do next except for me. I called the coroner, gave them the information they needed, and they came to take Crockett's body away.

My niece, Sonya, was really upset and decided to burn the recliner out in the backyard because none of us wanted the memories that the recliner held. It was the same recliner that Grandpa had used; he had left it empty and now Crockett had died in it. It was a very difficult time for all of us, especially our mother, who had now buried her two youngest children.

A few days later, there was a funeral for Crockett. Following the service, everybody drove in procession to the cemetery. We all gathered around the burial plot where a prayer was said before lowering the casket. After it was lowered, one of my nephew's friends walked over to "christen" my brother's casket by pouring a can of beer on him. As I saw this about to happen, I asked the director of the funeral home to say something to stop it. He did speak up, and my nephew's friend didn't pour the beer out. I hadn't wanted to be the one to say something because my nieces and nephews were already dissatisfied with the way I was handling Crockett's affairs, so I left it to the professional. My mother called my nephew and his friend a bunch of heathens, saying they lacked moral principles, and I agreed.

The family and friends gathered at his trailer after the committal service. A longtime friend of Crockett's, Mr. Brink, discreetly handed me something, and when I saw that it was money, I went into the bathroom so I could count it and put it away without a lot of people around. He had given me $400. I went back outside and thanked him for his generosity, telling him that I would spend it wisely. Mr. Brink said he knew that

I would do the right thing with the money. I only told my mother about the money, and after discussing it, we agreed that it would be best to apply it to the cost of the funeral. I put the money toward the funeral in Mr. Brink's name.

As per usual, my family started to stir up trouble with me right after Crockett passed away. My niece, Dawn, hadn't shown any concerns about me being Crockett's executor until two days before he had died. She had even asked me to pick up and drop off my brother's personal belongings at his trailer while he was still in the hospital, so I thought she was fine with my brother's decision to make me executor after she had declined. However, right before Crockett passed away, she changed her mind and wanted to take over.

Despite the fact that my brother was using morphine, she contacted a law firm, and they sent a paralegal to my brother's trailer to have a new will prepared that made her the executor. It is illegal to sign any legal documents while under the influence of any kind of drug, but the paralegal let him sign the new will anyway. I knew that this new will wouldn't be valid and that I was still the legal executor. Several days after Crockett's funeral, I went back to Crockett's trailer to pick out some things for my mom. Dawn had told my mom she could come and take anything she wanted, but she also knew that my mom lived 45 minutes away and didn't have a car. I took a picture of some deer, a watering can that I had given Crockett, and a hat he used to wear, all of which maybe valued $50.

About a half hour after I got home, there was a knock at my door. It was the police. I was on the phone with my mother at the time, so I told her the police were at the door and kept her on the line. He asked me if I was over at my brother's trailer and if I had removed some items, so I told him I had, and that I was planning to give these things to my mom for Mother's Day. I found out that Dawn had told the neighbors to call the police if they saw me go into Crockett's trailer because she said I was no longer Crockett's executor. After hearing my side of things, the officer left empty-handed.

A few days later, Dawn left me a message on my answering machine and said there was a warrant out for my arrest and I should turn myself in. I stopped by the Midland Police Station on my way to a support group meeting to ask if this was true, and they said it was, so I was arrested on the spot. I was taken to the county jail and held there for about 5 hours before Steve came and bailed me out for $200.

I had made bail, but my case wasn't dismissed yet. Just a few days later, I received a notice in the mail with a date and time for my preliminary hearing. I couldn't believe Dawn had taken it this far, but I wasn't going to back down. At my preliminary hearing, the judge conveyed the prosecutor's plea offer, which was either resisting arrest or assault. Both of those sounded worse than my actual charge of misdemeanor larceny under $200, so I was very puzzled when I turned to the judge and said, "Are those misdemeanors?"

He said "Yes," and hit the top of his desk with his gavel and told the court stenographer to enter a not guilty plea for me.

Eventually, I got a notice for another court date. I let my mother know and she agreed to go with me. It was nice to have my mother's full support for a change. We arrived to the court hearing early and I confirmed that my name was on the docket. While we were sitting out in the waiting area, an attorney came over and asked who I was, then he told us to sit tight and he'd get back to us. Forty-five minutes later, he came out and told us that we could go home. I asked him what had happened, and he just told me that the case was dismissed and walked away. I never did get an explanation. I'm assuming after further investigation on their part, they confirmed that the first will was the valid will.

I was glad I stood my ground. I was so tired of always giving my help and my time to people who asked, and getting burned in the end. I can relate to the saying, "Nice guys finish last." Despite the fact that the case was dismissed, however, I had a background check done on me by a possible employer. It said, "Motion for nolle prosequi is granted and the case is dismissed without prejudice," but it still showed that I had been arrested for larceny for less than $200 value. Even though my case had been dismissed and I wasn't convicted, it still looked like I was a thief, and that record prevented me from getting employment in the future.

Chapter 15: Prosecutors Perform Puppet Show

Now that Crockett's affairs were all taken care of, I needed to find a roommate temporarily until I got back on my feet. My son Steve introduced me to a man named Greg, who was looking for a place closer to his work, so I decided to allow him to live with me as my roommate. The living expenses would be split 50/50, and we would pay for our own phone and internet service.

Another benefit to having Greg as a roommate was he had some experience growing weed hydroponically, so we agreed that I would teach him how to grow in dirt and he would teach me how to grow in water. When our crop was ready for harvest, we'd split the proceeds 50/50 since we both were to do our share of taking care of the plants. Growing is a lot of hard work because the plants need attention daily.

While I was waiting to harvest my crop, I got a part-time cleaning job at an eye care center in Midland, which was very close to my gym. I worked evenings, and Greg worked during the day at a local restaurant, but I liked the arrangement because it gave us time to ourselves.

I didn't mind sharing my garden with Greg. However, he broke the first rule of growing. When I got home one day, Greg was showing the garden to a friend of his that I had never met before. The first rule of growing that I learned during my classes in Oaksterdam was to never show your garden to anybody, no matter how close you were with them. Once people see how well a garden is doing, the risk of them breaking in and stealing your crop increases. The local population of the area where I lived was full of seedy people. My neighbor referred to the area as "the land of the misfits." When the tourists that would come during the summer would leave, only the locals were left who were all considered country folk. They tended to drink and smoke weed all day long. I also knew there were meth labs scattered around the town.

There wasn't anything that I could do after the fact, but I did express my feelings to Greg and he assured me that he wouldn't take anybody else down there. A short time later, he told me that his friend decided he was going to grow. Greg then informed me that he was going to go over to his friend's house to help him set up his grow room. I could tell that there was something fishy going on; I thought Greg might teach his friend everything I had taught him about growing in dirt and then move out and start growing with his friend.

One morning, Greg came into the kitchen looking horrible, and I could tell that something was wrong. I asked him if wanted me to take him to the ER, but he said he would just go see his family doctor. He found out that he had a severe case of diverticulitis, which required surgery and a recovery time of about 8 weeks. Obviously, he couldn't work, so he wouldn't be able to pay his rent or other expenses. He thought it over and informed me that he was going to move back home with his mom until he recovered, which was understandable.

Greg was behind on rent payments, so he left me his hydroponic growing equipment and the rest of his growing supplies in lieu of rent. He had never taught me to use the equipment like he had said he would, but I was able to sell it. That was more than enough to cover what he owed, and I was fine with that.

A couple of days later, he called and said I could keep his share of the crop. We had been growing Acapulco Gold, which was the strain he wanted to grow. He reconsidered and called me back because he had no way of making money anymore. He had fairly contributed to my garden until he moved, and

I knew it wasn't his fault that he couldn't contribute anymore, so I gave him $300 cash – which was way more than he had expected.

I was living in my home in Beaverton alone, still working at the eye care center and growing medical marijuana. I came home from work about 10 pm one evening and noticed that my house, and the whole neighborhood, looked pitch black. As soon as I approached my driveway, I saw a huge tree lying on the ground. We had had a bad rainstorm and there was debris all over the place. I realized the power was out, and I didn't need that with a basement full of plants because they needed to be grown in a controlled environment. There wasn't too much I could do in the dark, so I just went to bed.

In the morning, I opened the basement door, and all I could see was water. I had forgotten that, without power, the subpump had stopped working too, and I didn't have a generator. The water was about 6 to 8 inches deep, deep enough that things were floating by. The only option I had was to bring my plants upstairs by the windows and into the natural light so their cycle didn't get messed up. I had about 14-15 plants in my flower room and they were at least at least 5 feet tall, so I called a woman, Carolyn, who I knew also grew. She and her husband Ted helped me: Carolyn and I waded through the water with a flashlight and one plant at a time to the base of the stairs where Ted took the plant and put it into one of my two bathrooms since there was no natural light in there after the skylights had been covered. That's where I kept them at night to keep them in the dark, and then I pulled all of them out at the crack of dawn so they could get as much daylight as possible. I didn't know if they would make it, but I had to try. It was three long days before the power was back on. Carolyn and Ted weren't available to help me move them this time, so I moved them, one by one, all by myself.

Fortunately, marijuana plants tend to be very resilient; they survived and made it to harvest. During harvest time, I had a friend of mine helping me trim the shade leaves before we hung the plants to dry. While trimming, I noticed that the plants didn't look the same; about half of them were different. I realized that Greg must have switched out some of the Acapulco Gold with whatever strain his friend had been growing. It was clearer to me why he had wanted to move when I wasn't home. I was right in thinking that something fishy had been going on when Greg invited his friend over; they might have had this plan all along. I couldn't be angry for too long though because I liked the other strain better than the Acapulco Gold.

I ordered some seeds from the UK over the Internet to get my next crop started. I had used this company before because they had a good selection and high quality of seeds. I was given the option to pay extra for a guaranteed delivery, but since I hadn't ever had problems receiving the seeds in the past, I opted out of the guarantee this time. The seeds never arrived, and when I called to inquire about this, I was told that I didn't get the package because I didn't pay extra for a guaranteed delivery. I didn't get reimbursed for the $227 I spent on the seeds, either. The next time I had to buy seeds, I decided that I would go pick them up in person.

While I was at a local dispensary to pick up some weed for myself since mine was still growing, the owner of the dispensary introduced me to a man in his mid-late twenties named Casey. Casey claimed that he smoked weed because of his Crohn's disease, but he wasn't happy with his current medical marijuana caregiver, so he wanted to find someone else. The owner of the dispensary suggested that Casey look at and sample some of my finished product in case he wanted me to be his new caregiver. We exchanged phone numbers prior to parting ways and he kissed me on the cheek nonchalantly and I thought that was pretty nice.

After a couple of weeks went by, Casey called and wanted to come over to my house and check out my medicine, so I invited him over. He liked what he saw and sampled, but then he started asking me lots of questions, such as which days I went to the gym, why my skylights were covered up, and if the storm windows in my living room were always foggy. I became suspicious that he was casing my house and my schedule so he could break in when I was gone, but I didn't know for sure.

He offered to help around the house in payment for the weed he'd sampled, and he was specifically interested in helping with "anything I might have in the basement." I really didn't need anything done, and I knew that he wanted to see my garden, but I wanted to give him the benefit of the doubt; if I was looking for a new caregiver, I would want to look at their plants as well to make sure they were healthy. Eventually, he persuaded me to take him downstairs and I knew in that moment I'd just broken the number one rule.

Before we parted ways, I asked to see his medical marijuana card and driver's license for proof of identification, and he flashed them at me briefly so I wasn't able to read either one of them. I didn't push the issue, but asked him for his last name and wrote down what he told me, and that was all of the information I had about him.

Another day, we talked on the phone and set up a meeting place in a Lowe's parking lot in Midland. When he finally got there a good half hour late, he was with another guy. Casey immediately got into my car and was under the impression that because his paperwork to legally make me his caregiver was in the mail, he was entitled to free medicine. I told him no, and until he had his new card in his hand, he wasn't getting anything from me; I wasn't his caregiver yet, and I wasn't going to risk losing what I had by providing him medicine.

On May 7, 2014, a beautiful day in Michigan, I drove to Traverse City to exchange some growing equipment that I wasn't going to use and buy some seeds to prepare for the next crop. I left early that morning and spent most of the day in Traverse City. I arrived home about 6:30 pm, and at about 8:30 pm, I closed the blinds for the night.

The morning came, and when I started opening my blinds for the day, I noticed the screens on my living room and bedroom window had been taken off. I could tell because they were put back in upside down and haphazardly. I also noticed some prying marks and scratches around the weather stripping of my back door. I called a friend of mine and told him that it appeared someone tried to break into my house, and I thought I should call the police and let them check it out. I was almost positive it had been Casey. My friend said that the police probably wouldn't do anything about it because the county was short-staffed on law enforcement in this area, so I didn't make the call, but I was still suspicious and fearful because I knew those marks weren't there before.

Two days later, nothing else had happened, so I went to my gym. I also planned on pricing security equipment after my workout. Prior to leaving home, my intuition suggested I put on a precious ring that I had received from Hugh 37 years ago. It was incredibly important to me, and I didn't want to take any chances, so I slipped it onto my finger and left my house.

I left around 12:45 pm and got to the gym at 1:13 pm. When I was done, I went to Best Buy and Meijer to look at what security equipment they had. I wrote down some info and left for home. It was about 3:45 pm and I was driving by the front of my home. I looked over to my left and saw that the screen from my bedroom window was off and the window was open. It looked like someone had come back, and they had waited until I had gone to the gym. Whoever this was knew my weekly schedule.

I was pissed. I sped up to get in and see what kind of damage had been done. I unlocked my back door and deadbolt and immediately dashed into my bedroom. There was broken glass lying on the carpet from the inside window, but the storm window was intact. I headed to the basement, where I knew I had probably been hit the hardest. The basement door was wide open. I went into the first plant room where my mother plants – the plants that I take the clones from, which were almost six feet tall – were fine. The plants that were in a vegetative state were also fine. Finally, I walked into my flowering room, knowing what I was going to find. The punk had literally ripped all of the tops off of eleven of my plants and took one whole plant, using my bag from Jamaica and my bathing wrap from Tahiti to aid in the process. Dirt was everywhere. I could tell that some of the pots had been kicked by the way the roots and the dirt were loosened from the pot.

My body was shaking; the feeling of being violated showed its ugly face once again. I was thinking to myself, "You have to call the police." I refused to live in fear. I called the cops and about 45 minutes later a deputy showed up. Just before his arrival, when I was making the phone call, I noticed my kitchen pantry door was ajar and there were drops of blood on the floor, on some plastic grocery bags, and on a cardboard box. The deputy asked me questions, filled out a police report, checked for fingerprints and footprints, took pictures, and took the DNA sample from my kitchen floor. I made sure that I didn't touch or go into a place where the intruder may have been so I didn't disturb any potential evidence. Once the deputy was done obtaining the DNA, I asked if he needed the bloody grocery bags or the cardboard box top, but he said he had what he needed. I decided to keep it anyway just in case.

A couple of months went by and not only was the deputy unable to find the suspect, but I was told the DNA wasn't obtained by proper protocol so they couldn't test it. I let the deputy know that I had kept the grocery bags and cardboard with the drops of blood on them, so he came by at midnight to pick them up.

I had a really strong feeling all along that this had been Casey's doing. Until the DNA test came back, I didn't know for sure who it was. Two or three weeks later, the deputy showed up and told me that the test results came back and showed that the DNA belonged to Casey. I was relieved that my suspicions were correct, but I was still pissed at that punk. All in all, I lost at least $7,000 and I had to pay more than $400 to replace the window because it wasn't covered by my renter's insurance. Casey had also taken several sentimental items that can never be replaced. I knew I was going to court over this matter.

There was first a preliminary hearing. I was called to the stand and was asked questions by both the prosecutor and the defense attorney. When the defense attorney had his turn, he asked if Casey and I had smoked marijuana together. My prosecutor just sat expressionless and didn't object to this question, so I looked briefly at the defense and then I turned my head toward the judge and said, "That's irrelevant, Your Honor."

The judge said, "Just answer the question."

I hesitated for a minute and said, "Yes."

They knew that I was possibly going to be Casey's caregiver, so sampling my product was a natural part of the process. After the hearing was over, I asked the assistant prosecutor why he allowed that question and he said he wanted to see how I would handle it.

It had been more than 18 months since Casey had broken into my house, and I'd been subpoenaed to court for a jury trial. The woman from the prosecutor's office, the victim advocate, was in the court room, but I didn't have any family or friends there. Prior to getting the subpoena, the head prosecutor asked me how I felt about a jury trial. I said, if that was what Casey wanted, all I had to do was tell the truth. His DNA was found in my house and he was willing to take a gamble with a jury. I was confident he'd be convicted. Regardless of what he stole, he'd still committed a crime and invaded my home. However, the court liaison that had been there to support me told me, "A jury can do funny things."

On Wednesday, December 9, 2015, court was in session at 9 am. I had four witnesses testifying on my behalf: the deputy that came to my home the day of the break-in, a 10-year-old boy who was fishing at the lake directly across the road in front of my house, the owner of the dispensary who introduced me to Casey, and the forensic expert who did the test on the DNA obtained by the deputy. Before the trial, a fifth witness came to my door and told me that Casey had been bragging to him about the break-in. I took the guy's name and number, but to my frustration, he was never subpoenaed to court.

When it was my turn to testify, I dressed in all black, with a nice professional jacket and slacks. I was sworn in and took the stand. The jury was sitting at my right, and they were allowed to ask me questions directly, which I later found out was illegal. I was asked to confirm my name and address, and then one juror asked if I live alone, which I also confirmed. Now the whole courtroom knew that I grew marijuana and where I lived all alone. I felt like a sitting duck.

The prosecutor, who was supposed to be defending me, questioned me after the jurors, and then the defense attorney was last. I was told to listen carefully to each question and answer without elaboration or argument. The prosecutor asked me things like how I divided my rooms up for growing, how I could tell when the marijuana was ready, how long it took to dry, and how the drying process worked. I felt like I was giving instructions on how to grow and cure marijuana, which had nothing to do with Casey's home invasion charge. The prosecutor claimed that the jury needed to be educated, but the focus of the prosecutor and the defense attorney was completely on the marijuana.

The more questions that were being asked of me, the more I started to hesitate to answer. I saw the direction this trial was going, and my blood started to boil. The assistant prosecutor never asked about the most pertinent information that the jury needed to hear, like the premeditated nature of the crime, and the questions Casey asked me about my gym schedule, the skylights, and the fogged windows. They didn't even mention the broken window in my bedroom. I felt like a fly caught in a spider's web; there was nowhere for me to go. I wanted to stand up and yell that those questions weren't relevant and spill all of the vital information that was being purposefully left out, but I thought I might be arrested for contempt of court.

The judge took about 15 to 20 minutes to give the jury incredibly confusing and stilted instructions, which essentially told them not to take the deputy's word as true just because he was a law enforcement officer. One woman on the jury even admitted that she was against marijuana, so I knew she wasn't going to be fair to me, but they still didn't dismiss her.

After my testimony, the court liaison who was supposed to be with me for moral support vaguely told me she had things to do and bailed on me. The court advocate wasn't there either because she had taken a family vacation to Disney World. My friends and family were working, so I stood alone once again to hear the final verdict.

About 30 minutes later, the jury returned to the courtroom. I wasn't feeling confident at all anymore; I knew I had gotten screwed. Therefore, I wasn't surprised when the jury had reached a verdict of Not Guilty. The jury didn't know that this was Casey's third offense, which would have made him a habitual offender.

The head prosecutor came over and escorted me downstairs to his office because he could tell I was ready to explode. The last thing the head prosecutor told me was, "Don't feel too badly about losing the case because Casey probably spent about $10,000 in attorney fees. If you see him around your place, call the police."

I was furious and just wanted to go home. I should have expected this. I wasn't going to get justice. After all, I was growing marijuana. They only cared about the weed. As I was driving home, my anger was building in my chest. When I got home, my kettle boiled over and the lid blew off. I used a technique I learned about years ago: I brought my arms up over my head, clasped my hands together, and beat the snot out of my pillow. Anger is stored in your chest, and this provides a safe way to release it.

After that, I took my Pitbull Brooke for a walk to relieve some more frustration. On the way back, Brooke wasn't even keeping up with me; I was still was steaming and needed to calm down. With my hands trembling, I rolled myself a big fat doobie. As I was smoking, I was pacing the floor from room to room, looking out the window.

I know the trial is technically over, but that experience totally destroyed any remaining faith I had in our justice system. I had abided by the law and only grew marijuana within the legal guidelines, and the very law that should have protected me as a victimized person let a guilty man walk. The prosecutors, and the advocate, and liaison all knew Casey was guilty, so I still wanted to know the real reason why he walked.

After asking around, I found out that Casey had told the owner of the dispensary lies about doing duct work in my basement to explain how his blood got in my house. The prosecutors, my defense, were both against the use of marijuana, and the owner of the dispensary was at risk of being closed down by them. Casey's family also knew a local judge, which suggested a possibility of nepotism. After I discovered all of this new information, I realized that I hadn't stood a chance.

I felt this had been a mock jury trial for upcoming cases involving marijuana theft since, according to my prosecutor, this particular court had never had one before. I was asked irrelevant questions and the main charge of the entire case was completely ignored. It's not okay for anybody to break into your home and get away with it, even if they don't steal anything. I've had traumatizing experiences with home invasion before, so I was devastated that the so-called justice system would push the trauma of having a man break into my bedroom to the side.

A week before Christmas, I was feeling vulnerable and emotional. I wanted the prosecutor and court liaison to see firsthand how the injustice of this experience had affected me, and wrote down some questions that I wanted answered. The assistant prosecutor had answers to give me, but they weren't the answers I was looking for. Tears were pouring down my face as I was telling them how I felt about the whole thing, they became defensive that I even questioned the quality of their work. When I was leaving, the court liaison asked me why I hadn't just left things alone. I told her that I was part of a trauma support group, so wanted to educate her and the prosecutors on the effects of being victimized.

Chapter 16: My Only True Love

Back in February 2014, I had taken a vacation to California to visit a few of the friends I had out there. I was still growing at this time, so I called a good friend who I trusted and asked him to take care of my plants while I was gone. I wanted to do my best to keep it simple and to a minimum, so I wrote down instructions and premixed fertilizers that were going to be needed.

I arrived on February 18, 2014 and planned to stay for 10 days. I rented a car and headed south to Lake Elsinore to visit Keith, and old friend who I went to elementary school with. He told me when I came to Southern California to let him know because he wanted me to come by and see his place. When I got there, I was totally exhausted, tired, and hungry.

The next morning, I was well rested and ready for the full day we had planned. Both Keith and I were going to see a friend of ours, Hugh, my ex-boyfriend from back in the seventies. I hadn't seen him in probably 36 years. Hugh and Keith had previously talked on the phone and we were all meeting at a pizza place for lunch, which was just a short distance from Hugh's place.

When I saw Hugh at the pizza place, we approached one another and hugged. He looked a lot different from when I'd last seen him. He was clean shaven with short gray hair and was pretty thin. I found out that he had Parkinson's disease. He was in the war in Vietnam and he thinks he got it from being exposed to the Agent Orange because nobody else in his family ever had it. Hugh said while his medication was working, he could function just fine, but once it wore off his body would freeze up without his medication.

After we ate, Hugh invited us over to see his home. He lived with his girlfriend, and she didn't use marijuana, so while she was at work, the three of us hung out in the garage and smoked some weed. We stayed for a few hours, but we had to leave before the traffic got bad. When Keith went in to use the bathroom, I felt compelled to get up and go over to Hugh. When I did, he stole a kiss and we hugged. I don't know what I was expecting, but it wasn't that. Keith came back without having seen us, and we both said our goodbyes to Hugh. As we were pulling away, I saw Hugh turn around and look back at me. Suddenly the tears came streaming down my cheeks from underneath my dark sunglasses. There was little conversation between Keith and me on the way home because my emotions were really stirred up and I was trying to be discreet. I hadn't expected to feel this way.

During the drive back, Keith said he was going to be working in Anaheim, so rather than driving back and forth from his house, he would rent a room in Anaheim and I could stay there. He was working third shift, so while he was working, I would be sleeping. It worked out well. Once he was done working for the week, he checked out of the motel and we went our separate ways. I planned to visit Robert in Long Beach before leaving California, but I wanted to visit Hugh one more time first, so I drove to Hugh's house.

When I arrived, we ate lunch and I gave Hugh a copy of my glamour picture, taken when I was 40 years old. We talked and clarified a couple of things from our past in regard to some of the issues that had caused us to break up so many years ago, and we made peace with those issues. I knew that I needed to get going. Hugh had been dating his girlfriend for 13 years, and she would be returning home soon. She knew I was in town, but we didn't want to make things uncomfortable for anyone, so I didn't want to stay too long.

Before I left, I asked him, "Do you love her?"

He responded, "She has a good heart."

It was time to say our goodbyes. I turned to my left as we were sitting in the front seat of his car, and he looked me in the eye. Whenever Hugh looked into my eyes, it was like lasers piercing into my very soul.

He said, "I love you."

I said, "I love you, too," as tears came shooting out and running down my surprised face.

Then he said, "Move in with me." I hadn't seen that coming.

We hugged again, and I said, "Goodbye."

He said, "Don't say goodbye."

I replied, "I'll see you later, then," and waved.

I got into my rental car and drove off, crying most of the way back to Long Beach.

I hadn't realized that I had these kinds of feelings until I saw him again. I was still in love with him, after all these years. I was trying to pull myself together while I was on my way to visit Robert, who I hadn't seen in four years. It was nice to see Robert; he's always been a positive, encouraging person to be around. We met up with some friends for Korean BBQ and I had a nice visit.

Even after returning to Michigan, I remained in constant contact with Hugh for the next three years. He would call me once or twice a week and tell me that he wanted to move back to Michigan and move in with me. He also said he'd pay me to take care of him, buy me a new car, and a riding lawn mower. All of that sounded good, but I only really cared about him and being able to spend time together. It wasn't until February of 2017 that I took another trip to California. I stayed at the same motel that I always did when I went to Long Beach, and I rented a car.

I was really excited and anxious to see Hugh again. I arrived at about 10:15 am and pulled in front of the house. Hugh had the garage door open and was waiting for me. We walked towards one another and he gave me a hug and a kiss. We stayed out in the garage where he had a CD player and some awesome speakers hooked up. He played some music and we smoked some good California weed. He made us some lunch, but my stomach was so full of emotion that I couldn't eat very much. After we ate, Hugh went over to his CD player and put in a disc; it was a new version of an old song, "It's a Man's World," done by Luciano Pavarotti and James Brown. As soon as I heard what song it was, I stretched out my arms towards Hugh and we embraced and danced. He was the perfect height that I was able to lay my head on his shoulder and his on mine. The whole while he was running his hands over the entire back of my body and I was trying to hold back my tears. It felt so good to be in his arms again.

Halfway through the song, Hugh softly said, "I love you."

I said, "I love you, too."

When the song ended, we stopped and stepped back and looked at one another and we were both in tears. I knew he didn't want me to see him cry, so he walked over to the side of his car and wiped his eyes as he tried to compose himself. Then he told me I should probably go so I could beat the rush hour traffic. We hugged again and I told him that I didn't want to let go, not knowing if I'd ever see him again. As my arms left his shoulders, the tears ran uncontrollably down my face. I turned and went to the car and waved to him as I slowly pulled away. I cried all the way back to Long Beach. That dance we shared was a very special moment, and one that I'll never forget.

A year later in early February 2018, I visited So Cal again and made plans to see Hugh. I flew out of the local airport, MBS, to the John Wayne airport in Santa Ana, California and rented a car. On February 6, I went to see Hugh. We were both anxious to see one another again. When I arrived this time, he made me breakfast and I ate while we visited. We had a nice visit, but I noticed that his Parkinson's disease was getting the best of him. When his medication would wear off, he would literally skip around when he tried to walk. I saw him twice during my week in California, but before I left this time, he gave me his Fender guitar, which he absolutely loved, along with some other sentimental items.

I asked him, "Are you sure you want me to take this?"

Hugh said, "Yes, I'm sure. I want to you to have it."

I know all too well what it means when people start giving away their personal items. He thought he wouldn't be alive much longer. This is how he puts it: "I'm going down."

Five months later, in July in 2018, I went back to So Cal one more time. I had still been in regular contact with Hugh. He had told me that he was ready to come back to Michigan and live with me. I was really excited because I had been waiting to hear this for the last four years. However, Hugh was still living with his current girlfriend, Gerri, of many years, and I felt really bad for her. Hugh claimed that Gerri wasn't taking good care of him, and he needed a lot of help because of his Parkinson's; he said she often complain about the amount care he needed. I wasn't able to confirm any of this because I'd never met Gerri, so I just took his word for it. In spite of this, I was also aware that Hugh would rather sneak around than confront any issues head-on. Regardless, we both knew that we were each other's one and only true love, and we were anxious to be together again.

Our friend Keith only lived about 30 minutes from Hugh. He and Keith had talked on the phone; the plan was that Keith would go and pick up Hugh and what luggage he wanted to bring with him and spend the night at Keith's. Hugh told Keith that he would pay for his round-trip air fare. Hugh needed Keith's help to get on and off the planes, so I wasn't planning on going unless Hugh thought that he needed more that Keith to assist him.

On Friday, July 27, Hugh called me and told me that he wanted me to come and get him. I immediately called a boarding place to see if they could take my dog, Brooke, last minute and then called the travel agent. I told Hugh that buying a ticket at the last minute was going to be extremely expensive ($1,357.80), but he didn't care about the money; he said he would pay me back for it. I put the plane tickets for Hugh, Keith, and myself on my credit card, a total $2,953.50. My flight was on Sunday at 5:30 pm. I had never travelled on such short notice before.

That Friday, Keith helped Hugh pack up his medication and clothes. Hugh's girlfriend, Gerri, was at work, and Hugh wanted to leave before she got home. I felt very uncomfortable about the way Hugh was going about this. I would have liked Hugh to have a conversation with Gerri about what he was doing. However, from my past experiences with Hugh, I knew that this was his way of handling things, and nothing I told him would change that.

Once they were in the car, Hugh told Keith that rather than going to Keith's place, he wanted to go to the local motel, which was 4-5 blocks away from where Hugh lived. When Keith called and told me Hugh's new plan, I felt less confident that Hugh really was going to leave California, but I had made plans to go and get him, so that was what I was going to do.

They checked into the room and stayed there for two days until I got there. Keith wasn't too happy about the situation; he hadn't realized just how bad Hugh was and the amount of care that he required. Hugh couldn't even get out of bed and use his walker to get to the bathroom. When I got there on Sunday, Keith picked me up from the Ontario airport and filled me in on Hugh's condition and needs. I had just flown almost 2,000 miles. I was excited to see Hugh, exhausted, and starving. When I got to the motel, Hugh was laying on the bed watching TV. I immediately walked over to him and gave him a hug and a kiss, and he immediately showed me an ounce of weed that he'd gotten for me. Keith said his goodbyes and was more than ready to go home. It was late at night now, close to midnight, and I really needed to sleep. I got myself ready for bed, and just about the time I was drifting off, I heard Hugh call my name. He wanted a drink. I got him some water and went back to bed. I started drifting off again and he did the same exact thing a second time. I was so overtired that when he called my name, my body twitched. If I had known he was this bad, I should have asked Keith to stay another night.

The next morning, at about 6 am, Hugh was wide awake and needed help to the bathroom. I needed more sleep. After I helped him and got him back to the bed, he dropped a bomb on me: He wasn't going back to Michigan, and he wanted me to hand him the phone. He said he was going to call his girlfriend Gerri and tell her where he was.

I asked him, "Are you sure this is what you want to do?"

He said, "Yes. I can't get on the plane like this."

I replied, "You had to have known this beforehand." I

don't recall what his response was to that comment. I think Hugh wanted me to see that he wasn't able to travel back to Michigan, but I also think he wanted to show Gerri that if he was able to leave, he would have left. Either way, it was an emotionally abusive thing to do, both to me and Gerri. I know that Parkinson's disease can sometimes also affect a person's mind, so I'd like to believe that his disease impacted his decision.

I gave him the phone and he called Gerri. He told her where he was and that he would have to call an ambulance to take him back home because she wouldn't have been able to get him into the car. After he called Gerri, Hugh said he didn't even want to visit with me; he just wanted me to go. I couldn't believe it. There was a Denny's restaurant right across the street from the motel. I was still very tired, hungry, and now very emotionally upset. Hugh gave me cash to pay me back for my and Keith's plane tickets, and then I walked to the restaurant and sat in a booth that faced the motel. I ordered some coffee and French toast. As I was trying to eat, I saw the ambulance pull up to the motel, and when they drove away, I knew Hugh was in there. My stomach was a mess. I was trying to eat and keep my tears from running into my food with each bite. I ate what I could, and then I walked back to an empty room, all alone. I didn't understand why the people who claimed that they loved me kept hurting me. I got on the phone and called Keith and told him that we would be flying back to Michigan without Hugh. I explained to him what had happened, and Keith and I agreed that Hugh planned it that way, which is why he wanted to stay at the motel. I didn't have a car, and my return flight was the very next day. I was an emotional wreck, crying in disbelief, and all I could do was hang around my motel room all day. I decided I really needed to smoke some of the weed that Hugh had given me. He had also given me a tube sock full of pure silver dollars that he wanted me to have. I also decided to give Robert a call and tell him what was going on. The whole time, I was sobbing and he knew I was very, very upset. After we talked, I laid down to try and get more sleep. That didn't happen.

I decided that if I wasn't taking Hugh home with me, I was at least going to take the good California smoke. I went to the laundry room in the motel and bought a package of dryer sheets. I put the weed in my plastic toothbrush holder and packed other things around it with the dryer sheets the night before I left. I figured that if I could smell the weed, I would have to do something else. I checked it first thing in the morning, and I couldn't smell anything. Finally, Keith called and said that he and his friend who was giving us a ride to the airport were on their way. When they showed up, Keith asked me about the weed. I told him that I sent it home.

He said, "What did you do, mail it from the office of the motel?"

I said, "Yes." (That would have been a great idea, but I didn't think about that; I was too emotionally upset.)

I didn't want Keith to know that I was smuggling it in my suitcase, so that if I got caught, he wouldn't be involved. We arrived at the Ontario airport and said our goodbyes to Keith's friend. We had some coffee before we headed to our gate to get checked in. Keith went through the X-ray machine first and put his carry-on on the belt. I went through next, put my bag on the belt, and when I got to the other side, a TSA officer pulled my bag off.

I immediately thought, "Oh crap. I might be going to jail."

The man unzipped my bag and was poking around looking at stuff. I walked over to tell him to please be careful because I had sentimental stuff in there, but he just told me to step back. I was trying to distract him. He pulled out the white tube sock full of half dollars. I told him that someone I knew had Parkinson's disease and he wanted me to have them. The whole time, my heart was racing. I just tried to remain calm and inconspicuous. After he looked at the coins, he put them back and zipped up my carry-on. I breathed a sigh of relief.

My flight home was fine, but I wasn't able to sleep. When we got to Michigan, Keith took my carry-on out of the overhead compartment. He could smell the weed at that point, so he asked me about it.

I told him, "Remember, my bag was pulled and searched in California."

He just said, "Oh yeah," and dropped the issue.

My car was in the parking lot at the MBS airport, so I drove Keith to his sister's house. I drove home to an empty house – again. I'm sure glad I had my dog, Brooke. She never let me down. I smoked weed and cried for the next few days.

After my failed attempt to bring Hugh back home and a broken heart, I decided that I needed to move on to the next chapter of my life. My intuition told me to get rid of the car I was leasing and move to Bay City and buy a house. By December 21, 2018, I closed on a small home and on December 26, Brooke and I moved in.

Even after a few years, this is still very emotionally hurtful to remember, but I still remain in contact with Hugh. I don't know how much time he has left and I don't want to miss any of his calls. Hugh is still with Gerri, but I feel bad for how much sneaking around he has done behind her back. He never talks to me unless Gerri is out of the house or taking a nap, and now that she is retired, I realize that I'll never see him again.

Epilogue

I am currently living alone in Bay City. I'm much happier here, and I feel safer. My Pitbull, Brooke was diagnosed with cancer in June of 2020 when she was 10 years old. As if I haven't had enough emotional pain already, I had to make the decision to end my dog's life. She was steadily losing her mobility in the following months, and I didn't want to let her suffer. I made an appointment for 4:00 p.m. on November 24, 2020, right before Thanksgiving. I was pacing the floor and watching the clock. At about 2:30 p.m. I hand-fed her an ice cream sandwich and took one last picture of her because she looked really content. At 3:30, we headed to the vet's office. When we got there, they said they had a room ready, so I took her in. They asked me to wait outside for a moment while they gave her a sedative, and then allowed me back in while they gave her the final shot. Once the shot was administered, Brooke took three short breaths, and then she was gone. They left the room and told me that I could stay as long as long as I wanted. I gave Brooke a kiss on her face and told her I was really going to miss her, and then I left. When I got home and opened the door, I saw Brooke's empty bed, and I started to cry. She was one of my greatest sources of peace and comfort, especially during the COVID-19 pandemic, and I miss her very much.

My mother, Mae, also lives in Bay City, only about 5 miles away from me. She doesn't drive anymore, so I take her to run any errands she needs to do. I have a complicated relationship with my mother. She has a long history of emotionally abusing and neglecting me. She is still hurtful with her words and actions, and is not emotionally available during any type of conversation, but I still spend time with her and try to do nice things for her. Regardless of how she's ever treated me, she is still my mother.

My relationship with my sister Deborah has been damaged since the loss of my boys. I keep her an arm's length away, and I keep personal things to myself. Conversation is superficial. But she is the only living sister that I have, and I do love her. She has had a lot of health issues and surgeries over the years. Again, regardless of past wrongs, I make it a point to spend limited time with her. She, my mother, and I will all get together on occasion as well. They might have hurt me and continue to do so, but I try to take the high road and still recognize that their lives have also been difficult and they are still my family.

My youngest son Steve is still living in Beaverton with his girlfriend as far as I know. Unfortunately, he and I have fallen out of contact for the past few years because of his relationship with his girlfriend, but I hope to hear from him soon.

In 2013, my oldest son Daniel was arrested for petty theft, but he was sentenced to time in prison because he was a habitual offender. On September 17, 2019, he was released on parole for a year, and completed his year without incident. I'm happy to say that he is currently employed, staying sober, and finally seems to be heading down the right path. Due to unknown circumstances, I haven't been in contact with him for a few months, but I hope he's doing well.

In September 2019, I went to Reno, Nevada to visit some family, and my best friend Norman and his wife Bonnie drove over from Northern California to visit me. We decided to meet at the Silver City Casino. When I walked into the casino, I saw Bonnie first and ran up to hug her, and when I saw Norman, I started crying; I hadn't seen him since I had left California in 1992 to come and take care of Grandpa, so I was incredibly excited to see him again. Norman, Bonnie, and I ate a delicious lunch and spent a few more hours playing keno and visiting with each other before I had to leave. I am happy I was able to see him again before the COVID-19 pandemic.

I'm still in contact with my friend Robert, and we check in on each other at least once a month. He got married a few years ago for the first time, and he still resides in Long Beach, California where he still works as a broker. Robert loves to take cruises, go to concerts, and eat at a wide variety of restaurants. He remains my good friend, confidant, and – if he had it his way – my financial advisor.

I am currently retired, and I'm done growing marijuana. It's too much work to grow it just for my use, and I've had too many bad experiences with growing it for other people to want to deal with it again. Now that it has been legalized in Michigan, I can buy it for a reasonable price.

I spend my time being an advocate and an activist. I have been my brother Kenny's guardian for 25 years, and I continue to advocate for his rights and the rights of all people with mental disabilities. I enjoy being an activist for causes that I am passionate about. In September 2011, I participated in a protest in Lansing, Michigan – the state capital – for the legalization of marijuana. In May 2020, I participated in a protest to support the Black Lives Matter movement after the murder of George Floyd.

One of the things I care deeply about is the awareness and empowerment of women because of my experiences, especially after the rape in Long Beach in 1989. Two years after the rape, I appeared in a documentary called "Crimes Against Women" in which I spoke about what had happened to me. Not long after, I gave an interview about the rape and it appeared on the front page of *The Long Beach Press Telegram*. I knew that many women stayed quiet about sexual assault and abuse, but I wanted my voice to be heard, and I wanted to help get rid of the stigma that our society still carried about women who have also had these kinds of experiences. I'm happy to see positive progression to erase this stigma due to things like the

#MeToo movement. I still intend on using my life experiences to help other women, and I would possibly like to do some public speaking.

I am still dealing with the repercussions of abuse throughout my years. It was difficult to be intimate with anyone for a while after the rape. The seed of fear from September 7, 1989 is still in my head and, obviously, it occasionally reappears. To this day, I'm very selective and cautious when considering a man who I may become intimate with, and if that man becomes too aggressive or doesn't stop when I ask him to, I simply won't spend time with him again.

On a lighter note, I try to spend my time doing things I enjoy and getting the best out of life. I really enjoy going to concerts, and I attend as many as I possibly can every summer. I also go out with my friends to dance and listen to local bands every once in a while.

My workouts are very important to me. For nine months, I was regularly working with a trainer at my gym four or five days a week prior to the COVID-19 pandemic. During the pandemic, I continued to work out at home four days a week. My initial reason for working out was to stay toned and to control my weight, but it has also been a good and healthy way to release stress and help me sleep. In addition, exercise helps keep my degenerative discs in my lower back in place. The last reason I like to stay fit is because if a man looks at me in a lustful way, I want him to know that I'm a fighter and I'm perfectly capable of defending myself regardless of how petite I am. I carry myself with my head up and shoulders back and walk with purpose. Exercise is a way to give me a sense of power and control over my own body, and it has helped improve my confidence and self-esteem over the years. I plan on continuing to work out regularly for the rest of my life.

Most recently, I have become an author. This is my first attempt at writing a book, so I've spent more than eight years writing this memoir. In doing so, I've been able to come to a lot of conclusions and realizations about myself that I hadn't before:

- I have not led a boring life.
- I haven't seen many happy times.
- One bad decision can impact a person's life – as well as the lives of others – forever, having a domino effect.
- Knowledge and education are key.
- Throughout my life, all I was looking for was love and my basic needs.
- I'm a survivor and I'm very resilient.
- I can be and have been able to adapt to different circumstances and situations.
- People who have found me physically attractive (men and women) oftentimes used this as an excuse to avoid me, stalk me, or abuse me.
- I've made a lot of bad choices in men. If they all would have left me alone and if I would have stayed away from them, I would have a very lucrative real estate career and a fat bank account for my retirement right now.
- I continue to give people the benefit of the doubt, even the ones who have wronged me.
- As the saying goes, you can count your **true** friends on one hand – my only true friends are Norman and Robert.

- I have endured a lot of physical and emotional pain due to the selfishness of others.

- In the words of Kelly Clarkson, what doesn't kill you makes you stronger, and I've become very strong.

- If marijuana was a gateway drug, I would most definitely be using harder drugs right now, but I'm not. I thank God every day for my weed.

- I enjoy writing and I have become a better writer.

- Despite knowing that the topic I had to write about would be painful and unpleasant, I knew that I would get through it and I would live.

- Writing this memoir has given me a sense of freedom and relief.

Thank you for taking the time to read my life's journey. With the knowledge I now have, I'd like to say a few things to you:

First of all, don't cheat yourself out of once-in-a-lifetime opportunities such as your high school prom or graduating with your friends, because once it's over, it's over. There's no second chance.

Second, remain chaste until you meet that special person; have self-respect and people will respect you. Also, if no one has educated you about safe sex, make sure to ask someone or find reliable resources that you can learn from. Don't try to have sex without knowing anything about the consequences.

Third, it's imperative that you take care of yourself first. I am not trying to sound narcissistic; I am trying to help you make smarter decisions. The fact of the matter is, putting yourself first is necessary. Only you are responsible for the decisions you make and the road you decide to go down. How can you expect to take care of or help others if you aren't able to take care of yourself?

Fourth, when you get into a relationship, just know that the first six months are the honeymoon period; don't make a permanent decision during this time. If you are thinking about having a long-term relationship with a person, get a criminal background check done on them, and also do your own personal background check by talking to their family, friends, or exes to make sure you know what you are getting into.

Fifth, when someone shows you who they really are, believe them. When the kettle is black, the kettle is black. If there are any signs of abuse or red flags, **do not ignore them**. Additionally, don't think that you will be able to change a person's behavior because you will trap yourself in an unhealthy relationship with that mindset. If abuse happens, acknowledge it and immediately end the relationship; if a person can abuse you once, they can and will do it again. I recommend that you get a good understanding of all facets of abuse as early as possible in life.

Sixth, if you find yourself trapped into an abusive relationship, reach out for help as soon as possible. This could be a relationship with a romantic partner, or even a family member or friend. I would recommend starting with a women's or men's shelter within your community; there are multiple support groups out there that are free to go to and can really help you heal and find other resources you might need to get out of that relationship. Make the necessary call. Tell a friend or go to your parents, but be sure to tell someone, regardless of the threats that the other person may have made to keep you with them. That's the abuser's way of keeping their power and control over you, so don't waste your precious life by staying in an abusive, toxic relationship. When it's time to move on, move on.

Charles Seindoll once said, "The longer I live, the more I realize the impact of attitude on life. Attitude, to me, is more important than facts…more important than the past, than education, than money, than circumstances, than failures, than successes… I am convinced that life is 10% what happens to me and 90% how I react to it."

I sincerely hope that you have learned something from my life's journey; I knew that my goal of finishing this book would be difficult, and I was correct in that assumption. While I writing this for the past eight years, I have relived the most painful experiences of my life, but it will all be worth it if, by doing so, you were able to learn from them. I hope that your life doesn't have the kind of drama that mine has had. I'll close by saying this: As Otto von Bismarck said, "Only a fool learns from his own mistakes. The wise man learns from the mistakes of others."

Acknowledgments

This book would not be what it is today without the assistance of many individuals who helped me along the way. First, I would like to thank Allison Brunner, who typed over 800 handwritten pages. Without her, my manuscript would not have made it into the hands of Helen Raica-Klotz, director of the Saginaw Valley State University Writing Center and Center for Community Writing. Helen's support and encouragement were invaluable as I continued to refine my writing. Through the Community Writing Centers, I received feedback and editing from Emma Chappel, who was willing to help me after work hours and on Saturdays. I also owe a huge debt of gratitude to Hannah Mose, another Community Writing Center tutor, for her hours and hours of dedication, patience, insight, and guidance. She helped to make this the best first book I could have hoped for. Yet another helping hand in this long, difficult process is Lizzy Kennedy, who provided excellent feedback on the numerous pages I submitted via email during the pandemic. I also received feedback on various stories from many wonderful tutors, including Josh Cianek, Darlene Carey, and Imari Tetu. Chris Giroux, assistant director for the SVSU Writing Center and Center for Community Writing, further encouraged my writing and provided feedback. Lastly, I want to acknowledge Sage Library, a branch of the Bay County Library System, where I discovered an advertisement for free tutoring. If I hadn't encountered the Community Writing Center and its staff, this would be a much different book.